BECOMING THE
ULTIMATE
PHYSIO

A PRACTICAL GUIDE TO PRIVATE PRACTICE SUCCESS

NICK SCHUSTER

"If there is one thing you need to invest in it is yourself."

Warren Buffett

"Succeeding in private practice requires much more than just technical competence. A careful and considered mix of personal character, professional will, leadership attributes, business acumen, and community endeavour must be blended with the more obvious contributions of clinical excellence and intelligent reasoning. Nick has realised this to be true for himself, and is one of the few members of our industry who is seeking to raise others' awareness to this. I encourage you to invest into yourself more broadly and with determination if you truly want to be effective."

Jason T Smith
Founder & Group Director, Back In Motion Health Group
Principal, Iceberg Leadership Institute
Chair, SOS Health Foundation

"As Physiotherapists our university education gives us an incredible understanding of anatomy, physiology and rehabilitation – however very few of us graduate with any business skills, marketing knowledge or how to make the most of our degrees and have a full and satisfying professional career. In this book, Nick lays out a blueprint for how to be a successful, effective and happy health professional. Essential reading for all current or future therapists wanting to succeed in private practice."

Paul Wright
Health Business Consultant
Director of OneMinutePractice.com and HealthBusinessProfits.com

"At its essence, being an effective and sought-after clinician requires clinical skills coupled with great communication. At its essence, being an effective practice owner requires far more. A greater impact beyond a sole practitioner requires team. Team requires leadership. Leadership requires intentionality, a commitment to mastering habits, garnering insights, making wise decisions, and both charting and staying the course. The best leaders in business are voracious in their pursuit of growing in their leadership. This can comprise investing into resources like this book to advance your leadership skill and capacity. Well done Nick on adding to the body of non-clinical helps inside the physiotherapy industry."

Brad Beer
POGO Founder, Physiotherapist, Bestselling author,
Host of "The Physical Performance Show"

"I can wholeheartedly recommend this book for physios considering purchasing a practice, for new clinic owners and even those who are experienced looking to grow. It is a thought-provoking book that challenges some of the 'norms' that hold back our wonderful profession. Use it with your teams, and pour over it a few times to glean all the gold nuggets of information."

James Schomburgk BAppSc (Physio), MAppSc (Manip Physio), APAM
Director Valley View, Campbelltown and Mt Barker

"In the last 13 years I have built The Physio Co into a practice that has eight times been ranked as one of Australia's 50 Best Places to Work. Looking back, the most important thing I have done to grow my business was to firstly grow myself. Regardless of any business goals, it's important that we focus on the big picture first – who we are and what we really want out of our work and our life. Learning to learn, to reflect and to become the best version of myself continues to inspire me everyday. I recommend you begin your journey of personal and business growth too."

Tristan White
Founder of The Physio Co
Author of *Culture Is Everything*

"Nick Schuster's passion for his patients and the profession of physiotherapy are clearly evident in *Becoming the Ultimate Physio*. Nick profoundly understands that operating a successful private practice requires much more than outstanding clinical competence. The lessons from his 'Physio Success Quadrant' should be required reading for all aspirational therapists seeking to optimise their professional success. In short, successful physiotherapy practice requires supplementing your clinical expertise with non-clinical education, ideally provided by those who have enjoyed success and learned the necessary lessons. Nick, in a very personal way, shares his success and provides a blueprint for its replication."

Gary Cunningham
Founder, Results Physiotherapy USA

"As a new graduate working in a private practice with two 10+ year experienced physios, I struggled to comprehend how I was providing similar value for patients as the other clinicians. To overcome this, Nick has challenged me for the last 18 months to grow not just as a physio but as a person. His approach to private practice is both patient and therapist friendly. *Becoming The Ultimate Physio* teaches you all the things you need to know about private practice that university doesn't."

Jackson Williams
Physiotherapist
Scarborough Physio and Health

"Being the ultimate physio is something Nick has worked towards throughout his entire career. He has worked tirelessly to educate himself and people around him, and his enthusiasm for helping people is outstanding. Nick has a high energy level, and is committed to improving the physio profession so that it is more recognised, more profitable and more professional. The information in this book is invaluable to anyone working in a clinic, anyone who owns a clinic, and anyone who wants to improve their practice."

Ruth Woollett
Practice Manager
Scarborough Physio and Health

"I have worked in private practice my whole physio career, and like many private practice physios I started to get complacent, unmotivated and just frustrated with the physio profession. I found I was just going through the motions and not excelling in my career. This was until I started working with Nick and undergoing the Ultimate Physio Training. I have never been so motivated and driven to be the best physio possible. The Ultimate Physio Training really has reinvigorated my passion for physio and has helped me get a better understanding of myself and my own barriers to success. I just cannot recommend this program enough."

Todd Bartholomew
Senior Physiotherapist
Scarborough Physio and Health

"In the last eight years I have sent hundreds of clients to Nick's practice to get treatment, with phenomenal results and feedback whether they worked directly with Nick or one of his amazing team. This guy is not only a great physio but a great leader, and most importantly a great person. Listen to what he has to say – he is the real deal, having built an amazing business."

Jake McLuskie
Founder & CEO of Positive Existence Personal Training

"Having known Nick personally for many years I can attest to his passion for personal growth and the business growth that follows. His relentless attitude and intellectual intensity grabbed me from our first chat on the touch football field.

To see his thoughts come together in this easy-to-read book is a gift to the young physios out there. Life is too short not to learn from others who walk the talk and hack their thinking! It takes someone willing to openly share. Within these pages, Nick shares all.

I encourage you to read and consider with an open mind, whatever health discipline you practise. As a dentist I got a lot out of it for myself and my team.

Authentic thought leaders are hard to find. For physiotherapy, Nick delivers."

Dr Dave Houston
CEO Australia Dental Group

"This book is a must read for all physios, from new graduates to senior practitioners. Nick's Ultimate Physio model is one of the most helpful mentoring and business development models that I have come across. Nick has been instrumental in helping me to value what I can offer as a physiotherapist and to improve as a practitioner. Thanks to Nick's methods, I am now working in my dream physiotherapy job while still maintaining a healthy work/life balance."

Shena Dale
Running Physiotherapist
Scarborough Physio and Health

"*Becoming the Ultimate Physio: the ultimate guide to private practice success* is a book that can benefit physiotherapists at all stages of their career. It challenges us to remember our purpose and why we became physiotherapists, and the importance of valuing ourselves, and the service we offer. For the new graduate, it offers advice for setting yourself up for success in private practice, and for employers, it's a reminder that your business is about the people you employ, as well as the people you serve. With increasing numbers of physiotherapists experiencing 'burn out' and limited opportunities for career advancement, it is critical we re-examine how we grow and support ourselves and each other to create a rewarding and sustainable career helping people. This is true for physiotherapists working in private practice, as well as other settings."

Cherie Wells
Senior Lecturer in Physiotherapy, Griffith University, Gold Coast

"I highly recommend all physiotherapists learn from Nick Schuster's message to value themselves highly.

I used to think that I had to be in physiotherapy just for the love of it, to the detriment of the rest of my life. This didn't match my focus of healthy activity and family life.

It was only when I valued my time and my skills highly that I could see how this helped me make the most of my abilities, allowing me to problem-solve even more effectively and create a better life for me and for my clients.

I also have a vision similar to Nick's: for physiotherapists to be valued similar to other successful professions. The good news is that it is already happening. The next step is for more curious physiotherapists to learn how they can also benefit themselves and their clients a lot more."

Michael Ridgway
Founder, Ridgway Institute International

"To be a great physiotherapist is one thing, to run a great physiotherapy business is something completely different, and to combine both is exceptional. Having known Nick for many years, initially as a friend and in more recent times a client, he is an exemplary model for anyone serious about building their business to serve their market and team in a truly valuable way. In his book *Becoming the Ultimate Physio*, Nick shares – in true abundant entrepreneurial spirit – real-world advice and guidance for other physiotherapist business owners on what he has learned and applied in building his own super-successful practice. This book is a must for any serious physiotherapy business owner."

Brad Flynn
Business Coach
Actioncoach International

ACKNOWLEDGEMENTS

Some of the incredible physio mentors I have had over the years include Michael Ridgway and David Butler from a clinical perspective, Paul Wright from a business perspective, and Jason Smith from a leadership and self-development perspective. All are experienced and progressive leaders in the field who started their careers as physios in private practice. They have reached amazing heights through their thirst for knowledge and learning – a desire you must possess if you really want to succeed.

After learning from these leaders I decided to pursue significant amounts of education in the business world. Some of the more significant business education I would like to acknowledge includes the Key Person of Influence 40-week brand accelerator programme run by Dent Global, and most importantly the business coaching which has changed my life courtesy of Brad Flynn, from Actioncoach International, which is a Brad Sugars company.

I would also like to pay tribute to the most inspirational business owner I know: Jake McLuskie from Positive Existence Personal Training. He has proven to me that one person can change the world if you think big enough.

If you are after some extra reading and resources, after completing this book I urge you to learn from the best, as these are the guys who taught me what I know, which has included some career-changing experiences. Find great mentors, and learn as much as you can from them. Don't hesitate to ask for their help.

DEDICATIONS

For Gerowyn and James for inspiring me at home.

For my team at Scarborough Physio and
Health for inspiring me at work.

First published in 2017 by Nick Schuster
Scarborough Physio and Health
93 Landsborough Ave
Scarborough QLD 4020 Australia

National Library of Australia Cataloguing-in-Publication entry:
    Creator: Schuster, Nick, author.
    Title: Becoming the ultimate physio.
    ISBN: 9780992480127 (paperback).
    Subjects: Physical therapy.
              Conduct of life.
              Well-being.
              Leadership.

Project management and text design by Michael Hanrahan Publishing
Cover design by Peter Reardon

Disclaimer

CONTENTS

Foreword   1

Introduction: The ultimate physio   5
Why did I write this book?   5
The problems with being a physio   8
My vision for physio   13
Physio is changing   14
The Physio Success Quadrant   17

PART I: YOU

1   How to be happy as a physio   23
What is happiness?   23
What is happiness to you?   24

2   Discovering who you really are   29
Personality profiling   29
The importance of being vulnerable   32

3   Playing above the bar   35
Above the bar   35
Below the bar   37

4   Be, Do, Have   41
'Do'   42
'Be'   44

PART II: PHYSIO

5 Why we need to redefine what we do   49
How should we define physiotherapy?   49

6 The resurgence of the manual therapist   53
Getting hands-on   53

7 Systematising your physio experience   59
The golden arches   59
What does my consultation process look like?   60
Process-driven thinking in a consultation   63

8 Making exercise prescription fun   67
Why do we prescribe exercises?   67
Personalising the exercise regime   68
Manual therapy plus exercises equals best outcomes   73
How many exercises should I prescribe?   76
Selling yourself to referrers   77

9 Nerves: the root of all pain   79
Testing neural tissue sensitivity   79
Referred pain versus compensation   82

10 Evidence-based practice does not equal research   85
What is evidence-based practice?   86
Using your clinical judgment   87

11 The diagnosis: key to the consult   91
A great practitioner is a good listener   91
Everything I do in a consultation, from start to finish   93

12 Being realistic about your level of experience   101
Ten thousand hours   101
Lower your expectations   103

CONTENTS

PART III: PEOPLE

13 **Improving your communication skills**   107

    The art of the perfect pitch   108

    Learn a new language   110

    The benefits of asking great questions   112

    Understanding your patients   115

    Providing strong recommendations   117

    Demonstrating empathy   120

14 **Dealing with your patients' problems and pain**   123

    Do you really know how they feel?   123

    Don't hurt your patients   124

    Handling patients' objections   125

    Challenging conventional thinking   126

15 **When do I see you again?**   129

    The variables in rebooking a patient   129

    My guidelines for rebooking   132

    To rebook or not to rebook?   133

    A plan for rebooking success   136

    Giving recommendations like an old hand   137

16 **Building strong patient relationships**   141

    Breaking the ice   141

    Good relationships are all about trust   142

    The customer is always right. Right?   143

    What do patients hate most?   146

17 **How to handle a dissatisfied patient**   149

    What do you do when your patient wants to break up with you?   149

PART IV: BUSINESS

18 **Being part of a strong team**   155
   The clinic owner's perspective   155
   Being happy, happy, happy   156

19 **Ideal clients and raving fans**   159
   Who are your ideal clients?   160
   Create raving fans   162
   How to sell yourself to a patient   169

20 **Handling the money side of things**   173
   Talking about money   173

21 **Physios and marketing**   179
   Why physios need to market themselves   179
   How to become known in your community   180
   Finding your niche   182

22 **The importance of networking**   185
   Professional isolation and what to do about it   185
   Never stop learning   186

23 **Bring it all together**   189
   So, what next?   190
   A better future   191

FOREWORD

As the CEO of the peak body for the profession, I continue to admire the contribution that physiotherapists make to the community.

Quite often, they are unsung heroes – always happy to take a back seat whilst their craft is administered to millions of Australians each year.

There are just over 30,000 registered physiotherapists in Australia and each one of them has a thirst for knowledge, strives for clinical excellence and, most importantly, is solely focused on the health and wellbeing of the consumers of their services.

Physiotherapy does not discriminate and has amazing cut-through in our society.

At times, I'm in awe of the power of the profession.

There are so many challenges and opportunities in the current Australian healthcare system, which isn't perfect, but by global standards is well regarded. From my perspective, unlocking the power and reach of primary care physiotherapists will enable the system to operate more effectively and efficiently, and potentially alter the health profile of Australia permanently in a positive way.

A record number of young physiotherapists are entering private practice – this can be a daunting but very rewarding experience.

The private practice of the future will exhibit a number of qualities. Our research at the APA suggests the critical factors for future success include offering a broader range of services, focusing on the consumer and outcomes, being responsive to the changing needs of the workforce, possessing business acumen, connecting with technology and, finally, partnering in teaching, training and research.

To this end, the value of lifelong learning for all healthcare professionals cannot be emphasised enough. As part of a profession based on safety and quality, the desire to learn and to continue to improve is critical in upholding the collective "brand" of physiotherapy that has been carefully developed for over 110 years in Australia.

When I reflect on my ongoing leadership journey, there has never been a 'light bulb' moment where leadership has simply turned on. In my view, the ability to keep an open mind is just as important as formal education, a broad range of experiences and strong peer and mentor support. However, my biggest leadership lessons have always come from volunteering experiences on various committees, groups, organisations and NFP boards. The lessons that are learnt from these settings are so rich and have great application across so many environments. There is a huge demand for volunteering in Australia and it can provide you with so much in terms of leadership and becoming the Ultimate Physio.

I applaud and admire contemporary physiotherapists like Nick who have a thirst for ongoing self-improvement but, more importantly, are willing to impart their knowledge to others within the broader physiotherapy community.

Enjoy the read. I urge all health professionals and consumers to continue being vocal advocates for physiotherapy in Australia.

Cris Massis
CEO
Australian Physiotherapy Association

THE ULTIMATE PHYSIO

WHY DID I WRITE THIS BOOK?

As an experienced physio I have come across some incredible people who have also chosen the physio profession, from the best and brightest young minds in our country, to the young up and comers forging a pathway and creating new models and concepts within our profession, to the experts at the top of their game teaching us all how to be better physios.

I have identified that the vast majority of us chose physio for one reason: we love helping people. We could have become doctors, dentists, lawyers or businesspeople. But we put our desire to help people and to be the best physios we can be above money, status, social rewards and prestige.

FOR PHYSIOS ...

But there is a problem with this. Physios in Australia today are more disillusioned than ever. We operate in a significantly "bottom heavy" model where you reach your maximum potential very early in your career. This is leading to physios working very hard, not seeing adequate rewards for their efforts, and thinking, "Is this all there is?"

At what stage of your career does this happen? For some people this happens after only five years, but the evidence points towards a strong dropout rate between the ages of 35 and 40.

I don't feel like this.

Why?

I have done more work on myself than on my technical skills.

You will spend so much time during your physio career caring for and helping other people that sometimes you will forget to take care of yourself. I am a naturally selfish person. What a terrible thing to be… or is it? Consider this radical concept: what if you took care of yourself first, then you could take better care of your patients and all of the other people in your life?

When you fly, the airline cabin crew will tell you in an emergency to put your own oxygen mask on first before trying to help other people. So why do we as physios try to put everyone else's masks on before putting our own mask on, and end up suffocating as a result?

If you are not happy it is nearly impossible to be great at your job and also be satisfied and fulfilled in your life. In this book I will teach you how to be the best physio you can be and, more importantly, to be the best person you can be, which is the basis for living a life of purpose.

My goal is to create career physios. Ultimate physios. I have never liked the concept of changing careers six or seven times in your life – I feel it's a waste of precious time and skills. Why not enjoy what you already do better and put that experience to good use?

FOR CLINIC OWNERS ...

So you are a clinic owner. You have a team of physios, a solid business, and a stable caseload of clients who sing your praises. You know what you're doing, right? How can this book help you?

If you are the type of clinic owner who takes personal and professional growth seriously then I believe this book has much value for you and your team members. If you are anything like me, you are far from perfect. You have learned to do everything your way, which may work for you but is not necessarily the best way. Sometimes you can find that as the clinic owner no-one challenges you because you are the boss, but I have personally found that the more my team members challenge me, the more I grow and improve as a leader and – more importantly – as a person.

This book will help you become a better physio, a better businessperson and a better leader. I have learned that leadership starts with you – if you are not in charge of yourself, should you really be let loose to be in charge of other people? You need to learn more about yourself before you can be a great leader, and this is an area where many of us fall down – we try to fix everything and everyone around us, without fixing ourselves. This book will make you consider some of these deeper issues that you face every day in a completely new and different context. I have been thinking this way for about five years now, and I firmly believe that to be the best physio I can be and the best clinic owner I can be I need to become the best person I can be.

My experience has led me to determine that most physios – and especially younger physios – have the same challenges, and this book will help you to identify and overcome these.

This book can also help your team. I'm sure that as a business owner you always have a million things on your plate (I'm in that situation too), and you likely cannot give your team as much time as you would like to regularly mentor them, help them manage their complex patients, and generally listen to their problems and challenges.

THE PROBLEMS WITH BEING A PHYSIO

I have been a physio for 14 years. I love what I do – the rush I get from seeing people at their worst, helping them with a major health problem which is holding them back physically, mentally and emotionally, then seeing them grow as their pain recedes and they return to normal life is one of the best feelings I get in my daily life. But, I often feel I am one of the lucky ones. You see, there's a major problem with physiotherapy today. This is the problem that causes physios to leave our profession in droves: our career peaks very early, and does not progress exponentially like most other professions.

Let's have a look at the typical career path for a physio. When I studied physiotherapy I lived on campus at the University of Queensland in a residential college, which I loved – I enjoyed the study, and the lifestyle was great. There were so many bright and aspirational people studying all sorts of degrees: law, pharmacy, business, accounting, engineering, dentistry and medicine, among many others.

We studied these degrees in parallel, and we all looked forward to graduating, entering the workforce, and proving ourselves in our chosen profession. However, in my final year of physio I started to have doubts about my chosen career. I heard the law students talking about getting their first job as an intern, working their way up as an associate, then senior associate, with the aspirations of eventually taking on partnership in a law firm. The medical students talked about being a resident, and then a registrar in a hospital, then a qualified doctor, then potentially specialising in their chosen field of medicine. This made me think – when you graduate as a physio, what's next? Where do you go from there? There are no different tiers within the physio profession, and no corporate ladders to climb. You are either a physio or … a physio.

After starting my career I became acutely aware of this. The first couple of years I learned so much, but I did feel like I was slipping into a comfortable groove, like my favourite chair. The problem with getting into a comfortable groove is the danger of becoming *too* comfortable. So, I started observing physios all around Australia when I did my professional development. There were junior new grad physios, mid-level physios, and experienced physios.

Many of the experienced physios I met seemed to be quite jaded. They were generally clinic owners or senior physios in their places of work. They worked very hard, and often seemed overwhelmed by the volume of work they had to do – treating the patients and taking care of the business and staff. On top of this they were responsible for office administration, balancing the books, building referrer relationships, replacing staff who left (all too often, it seemed), and somehow having a personal life also.

The next bit struck me pretty hard. When leaving the conferences I would get in my beat-up Mitsubishi Magna, and I would look across and see some of these more senior physios driving cars similar to mine. Speaking to these dedicated physios, their income didn't seem to reflect the amount of energy they were expending. On further investigation I found that these very capable physios were only charging a tiny bit more than me for a consultation in their clinics.

After going to university with all of these students who were going into professions that charge rates upwards of $200 per hour in medicine, engineering, accounting and law, I soon saw that physios were caring and charitable people who seemed to provide care at the expense of their own happiness. These people did not value themselves enough.

What makes things worse is that our profession has no clearly defined career pathway. If you do happen to follow the speciali-sation pathway that the Australian Physiotherapy Association has outlined and you become a specialist physio then you may feel you have earned the right to bump your consultation fees up, and I agree that you have that right, but do your patients understand your extra qualifications and why you are charging more? The average person understands the tiered-fee difference between a GP and a medical specialist, and also the fee difference between a solicitor and a bar-rister, but not one person I have surveyed fully understands the qualification difference between a physio and a specialist physio.

This leads to us as physios continually having to justify to our patients, and more importantly to ourselves, why we try to charge fees that are above the average expected fees within our profession, and this can wear you down after a while.

SO, WHAT DO WE DO?

When the profession you work in does not have a progressive career pathway, you have three options.

The first option is put up with the status quo. You will work your career away as a physio, be happy some days and not others, but my biggest concern for you is you may finish your career won-dering about what may have been. Was there a better way, could you have done something differently, or should you have chosen physiotherapy at all?

Option two is to quit and try something else. Move on and study medicine; completely change your career; go and perhaps sell your soul and become a medical sales rep to earn more money, or try to create wealth and financial security through traditional means such as investing in property and shares like everyone else does. If this is you, maybe you will feel that you shouldn't have been a physio in the first place or that it was a good stepping stone to somewhere else, but the physiotherapy profession has likely been robbed of a potentially great physio who had the potential to influence people's lives for the better.

Option three is my favourite: learn to know yourself and what you stand for. Learn to value yourself. Once you value yourself and your unique knowledge you are more likely to find your calling and add value to thousands of people's lives. When you are adding value to people's lives you can evolve your physio career into something that works for you, and it helps you to see the unlimited possibilities available to you working in an evolving profession like physio.

Option three is what *Becoming the Ultimate Physio* is all about.

BY THE NUMBERS

I want to start explaining how bad the problem is in our profession by throwing some stats at you from the Australian Government Job Outlook page.[1] This page gives demographic information about different professions, and I compared the physiotherapy profession against the mean. The mean age of a physio in Australia is 35, compared to the mean average of a worker in any occupation, which is 40.

Let's look at these figures in some detail. The average split for an occupation in Australia for workers aged under 45 versus workers aged over 45 is a 60–40 split, which means 40% of workers in the average occupation are over 45 years old. In physio, this split is 80–20, which means that only 20% of people working as physios in Australia are over 45. So what happens to your career when you reach the age of 45 that makes so many physios leave the profession? Let's use medicine as a comparison: 42% of medical practitioners are aged over 45. What about law? The figures show that 37% of solicitors are over 45. And 31.6% of accountants are over 45. So either our profession is killing us or we have such a great

---

1   http://joboutlook.gov.au/occupation.aspx?search=alpha&tab=stats&cluster=
     &code=2525&graph=AG.

desire to retire at age 45 that few of us physios make it in our career past that age.

But, there is one other way to interpret this statistic, and this is that our physio job market is being flooded with graduates. I believe this is definitely the case. When I graduated in 2003 from the University of Queensland, we were the only physiotherapy university graduate cohort in Queensland. Currently in Queensland there are two physiotherapy university courses in Brisbane, two on the Gold Coast and one in Townsville. I could extrapolate this to estimate that there are approximately four to five times as many physios graduating now compared to 2003.

In a job market flooded with young physios but without a clear career pathway, we have been significantly lacking leadership in the private practice space. There is a group within the APA called Physiotherapy Business Australia, but this is the only private practice–focused group, and this group is almost specifically geared towards business owners.

There are certain leadership programmes available through physio franchise groups here in Australia, which I have completed and have found beneficial. While I'm glad that I came across these professional and personal development programmes, I am surprised at the lack of non-franchise staff completing these courses given the high quality of the material.

My intention is to bring all of these issues together for you as the reader. (And I would like to be guided by you as to whether the material in this book is beneficial, and what else you want and need to know in the future, as I don't plan on stopping here – the next step is adapting this material into a practical course.)

Becoming aware of what you need to do and who you need to be is the first step in becoming the ultimate private practice physio, but hands-on experience and living it is the essential step to make the necessary transformation to leading yourself, your patients, your fellow physios and your community. Let's go on this journey together, and form strong bonds with like-minded physios with the benefits of promoting our profession, differentiating ourselves from the chiropractors, osteopaths, exercise physiologists and massage therapists, and most importantly living a life of happiness, significance and purpose.

MY VISION FOR PHYSIO

They say in business you have to have a vision. The purpose of a vision is to be able to lead from the front, make good decisions in alignment with achieving your vision, and inspire people around you to share in your vision.

Does the physiotherapy profession as a whole have a vision? The Australian Physiotherapy Association's vision is a good one – that the whole community recognises the full benefit of physiotherapy (from their 2015–17 Strategic Plan). But what does this look like? The clearest way to define what a vision is is to close your eyes and imagine a real-life situation that mirrors your vision.

I have a vision for physiotherapy in the private practice setting. Customer service surveys I have performed with current and previous patients in my clinic have told me that 9 in 10 people come to my clinic for pain relief, for a number of different injuries and complaints. My vision for physiotherapy in private practice is simple – that a person in pain calls a physiotherapist for help, rather than any other profession. Simple, but achievable.

Currently, when people are in pain they may call a GP clinic, physio, chiropractor, massage therapist, acupuncturist, osteopath, or many others. I believe we as physios are best equipped in terms of our skillset to be first-contact practitioners for people in pain. We have very thorough assessment skills and familiarity with a wide range of neuromusculoskeletal and general health conditions which allow this. In the modern Australian health landscape of shorter

GP appointments, we have the real ability to help get to the bottom of why our patients are in pain, and to make a real difference to their lives. Generally we are also really great at referring on when needed for further investigations and GP or specialist intervention.

My vision has a second part, and this is relating to my statements above regarding physios not valuing ourselves sufficiently. When we don't value ourselves it's hard for our clients to value us. Conversely, doctors value themselves. They study long and hard to get where they are … and don't we know it! The confident way they communicate with their patients leads me to believe that they value themselves, and hence their patients value them – their advice, their recommendations and their time.

My vision is for us as physios to be valued in society in the same way doctors are valued. This is a big vision, and it must start with us. We have so much to offer to people suffering pain and injury – we just need to believe it and communicate it confidently to patients.

PHYSIO IS CHANGING

Physiotherapy is a very young profession – in its current form it has only been around for approximately 100 years. For the bulk of those years, physios worked in hospital-type settings.

When I finished my physiotherapy degree at the University of Queensland I was part of a graduate cohort of approximately 80 people. The bulk of our training was geared towards working in hospitals, as was the bulk of our final prac year of work experience. We had a reasonable amount of training in musculoskeletal therapy, but not really enough to be confident in a private practice upon graduation.

I really didn't feel well prepared to work in a private practice when I graduated, but I got by. I'm not sure if you have had these feelings as well, but among other physios I know who work in private practice I'm certainly not alone.

At university there is not much mentioned regarding private practice. In saying this, we do have a very good grounding in anatomy, biomechanics, and everything you need to be a good physio, but we have no grounding in how a private practice actually runs, the different elements of private practice, how to succeed in this setting, and how some of the skills we require to succeed in private practice are different from those in a hospital.

One very basic concept of hospital versus private practice that is distinctly different is the concept of patient discharge, which is a hospital philosophy and some would say the main goal of your intervention with your patient in hospital, versus a patient becoming a lifetime client in private practice, and you see them for help with various injuries and ailments throughout their life. If more young physios were trained in relationship building at university this would dramatically increase their chances of success and satisfaction early in their private practice career.

The physiotherapy profession is changing. The majority of physios these days are employed in private practice. Our training needs to change to reflect this trend, to make sure the physios of tomorrow know how to succeed in private practice.

MENTORING IN PRIVATE PRACTICE

For the first five years of my private practice career I didn't have a mentor. I have now been a physio for 14 years, and I have had four different mentors, and this number is growing every year.

Like many students, when I first graduated I was naive but I thought I knew everything. How wrong I was! Straight after graduating from your degree you will have brass confidence. But you are given a harsh reality check when you start your private practice career.

The benefits of having a mentor as early as possible in your career are significant. A good mentor will help to accelerate your development as a clinician, will help you develop the "bedside manner" that is so sorely needed when dealing with members of the public who are seeking your services for advice regarding their health issues, and very importantly, will assist you to avoid making the same mistakes that they made as a junior practitioner.

When I was a young physio I tried hard to help people with their problems. I did lots of research into their conditions, I did several professional development courses every year to learn new techniques from the experts in my profession, and I had a thirst for knowledge.

If I had a mentor then I would have had an expert directing me in my professional development, and steering me towards the courses that were most valuable to me. But most importantly, I would ideally have had someone who was in the next room over from me throughout the day – someone who I knew was looking out for me, who I could bounce ideas off, who I could discuss my challenging patients with, who would motivate me and guide me towards a common vision and set of goals.

This is the mentor that I am trying to be to my staff today. It is a role I greatly enjoy. The vision of our clinic is for the Redcliffe Peninsula – the beautiful area where our clinic is located – to be the healthiest and best place to live in Australia. I firmly believe in this vision, and I work hard to make sure my staff act on a daily basis with this vision in mind.

When you are looking for a mentor, you need to make sure that your chosen person has shared values with you. If your mentor is a hard worker, you need to be prepared to work very hard. If your mentor is unwavering in their ethics, you had better be the same. If your mentor is visionary with lots of great ideas, you need to impress them with ideas of your own.

Conversely, if your chosen mentor does not have the qualities you wish to develop as a private practitioner, I would advise you to seek out someone who does. There are plenty of wonderful private practice owners and physios who would be happy to share their wisdom and experience with you.

I do believe that our busy daily workloads are definitely a barrier to the mentor–mentee relationship. But this is just the practicalities of working in a business. Often the more mature the business, the more time for mentoring the practice owner will have. Practices that are in their infancy, or alternatively in phases where they are undergoing growth or expansion, require young physios to work more independently on a daily basis.

I always wish I had more time for mentoring with my staff. But sometimes I look at my diary and one of my loyal patients has just hurt themselves, and needs my help. Sometimes I have to put out a small "fire" at work, as we practice owners need to deal with so many operational issues in our businesses: landlords, rent, phones, insurance companies, salespeople, accountants, the major health funds … the list is as long as my arm.

THE PHYSIO SUCCESS QUADRANT

As an experienced physio, business owner and people person, I am going to introduce you to the four key areas in which you need to be successful to be the consummate professional in the private practice setting. This concept is called the Physio Success Quadrant. We will be revisiting this throughout the book. The four key areas are:

1 **You**

2 **Physio**

3 **People**

4 **Business.**

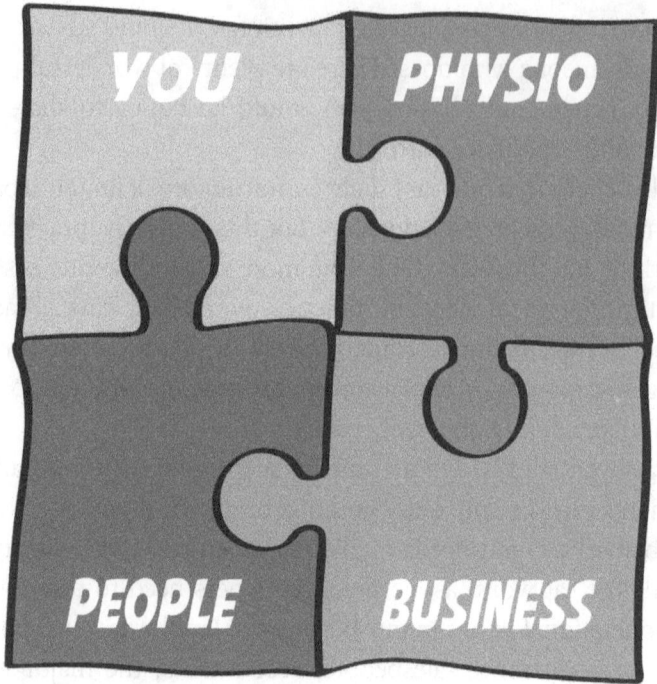

Only when this powerful quartet comes together can you be a truly successful private practice physio. Proficiency in two of the key areas will make you a good operator, but it is only those who can master all four who will become highly successful physiotherapy practitioners, with a long and growing list of patients waiting to see you.

Many physios I know are good at either physio and people, or physio and business; in fact, I believe the bulk of physios are proficient at two areas. It is rare for a physio to be good at physio, people *and* business. These people are generally the leaders in our industry, owners of large clinics and drivers of our profession. Very few of us are aware of the existence of the first point: you. I believe the key area of *you* is where we all must start, and without this falling into place the others are useless – like a map that gets you to the wrong place because your starting point was wrong.

I will teach you inside knowledge on each of these four areas, and I will expand into serious detail to answer the burning questions which I'm sure are floating around in that health practitioner brain of yours.

Why do I do what I do?

I love physiotherapy.

I mentioned earlier the incredible feeling I get from helping someone overcome a complicated health problem. The more people you help, the better your life becomes. The happier your life becomes, the more people gravitate towards you and the more lives you positively influence. From this influence comes opportunities, new ideas, partnerships, relationships with key people of influence, and satisfaction in your profession and your life that you did not think possible.

Oh, and I forgot to mention, quite a nice living as well. After all, we all have to put bread on the table, don't we!

So, let's get into it …

PART I

YOU

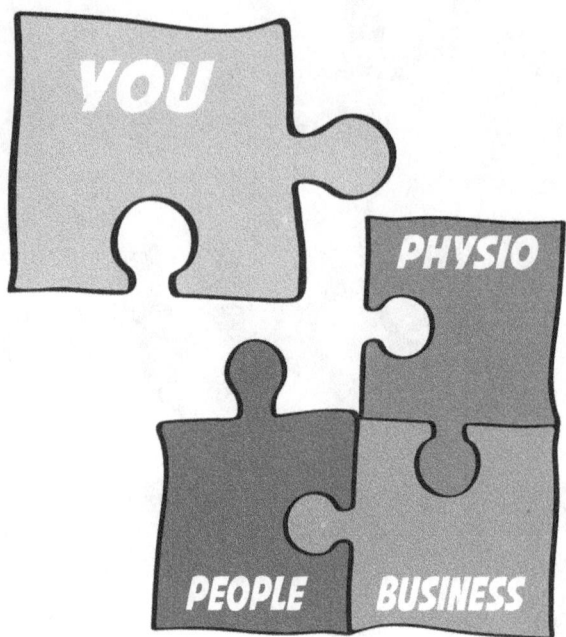

CHAPTER 1

HOW TO BE HAPPY AS A PHYSIO

WHAT IS HAPPINESS?

What *is* happiness? It can be many things, and it can be defined extremely broadly: some people want status, others want success, money, time, to be loved and adored, and so many other things. The list of possibilities is endless.

During my many conversations with my business coach about happiness, we have agreed that being happy coincides with living in a state of peace and spending as much of our lives in the present moment as we can. But this is often the hardest thing to do in this modern life of distractions, worries, stresses, fears and uncertainties.

Being happy for me is a choice that I make every day, but I have also learned it is impossible – and even unhealthy – to be happy all the time, or to strive to be happy all the time.

I would also differentiate between being *positive* and being *happy*. I take a positive mindset into my day, but – like you – I have things come up during the course of an average day that challenge me, surprise me, distract me, and generally detract from my state of happiness.

As physios we have some obvious things that should keep us happy: our patients, our relationships with them, the positive results they achieve with our intervention, and how this makes us feel. Compared with many other professions where you don't have as much personal interaction or nurture such meaningful and lasting relationships, we are in a really good situation. I know many doctors whose day is usually littered with trauma, tragedy and suffering. I would not want to be a doctor for all the money in the world.

WHAT IS HAPPINESS _TO YOU?_

If you are striving to be happy in life, the first thing you need to do is determine what happiness actually means to you. I'm happy when I am living by my highest values (I explain below what this means to me). Doing what you love is another way of explaining this, although sometimes it's hard to be able to do exactly what you love as a profession. I love golf and surfing, but I sure as anything am not that great at either, and could not earn a living from these things I love doing.

Two things that stop many people from being happy are their own limiting beliefs and not living according to their values. Let's have a look at each of these.

OVERCOMING YOUR LIMITING BELIEFS

Don't believe everything you think. This statement has never been far from my thoughts ever since I truly learned what it meant. It's possible that your thoughts are actually holding you back. Let's see what you can do about this.

I have a great mentor; he is my business coach and his name is Brad Flynn. I owe much of my success to his teachings. One area that Brad has drilled me on over the years is becoming consciously aware of limiting beliefs. It never ceases to amaze me how many limiting beliefs I have, and when I meet other physios and speak with them I can see how their limiting beliefs affect their progress as well.

An example of one of my biggest limiting beliefs as a clinic owner of a multidisciplinary allied health clinic is the mistaken belief that "no-one can do physio as well as me when it comes to my patients". This is a belief that most clinic owners share, and as your physio career progresses and you help more and more people, your great results with your patients can further feed and strengthen this limiting belief.

Let's now consider the most commonly held limiting beliefs that physios have, especially early in their careers:

- The patient does not value what I have to offer due to my lack of experience.

- I can only provide value if I do heaps of manual therapy and give heaps of exercises.

- My patients won't want to give me their hard-earned money for what they may consider to be a service inferior to that of a senior physio.

I have identified these three beliefs as the most common limiting beliefs in the clinical lives of young physios I have mentored, employed and surveyed. The problem is these beliefs will reinforce themselves as we find examples of where they are true in our lives. There is, however, a way to blow these beliefs out of the water using the following exercise.

Exercise: Overcoming limiting beliefs

Here is my step-by-step process to overcome a limiting belief:

1 Identify the belief and write it down.

2 Write down examples of when this belief has been true in your life.

3 Write down examples of when this belief has been untrue in your life. Find more examples of when this belief has been untrue than when it has been true.

4 During your clinic practice, identify specific occasions when your limiting belief is being proven to be false – this will happen regularly once you are aware of what the belief is.

DISCOVERING YOUR HIGHEST VALUES

One thing has changed my career and my life in a more significant way than anything else that I have ever learned. This one thing has given me purpose, made me happy, helped me understand who I am and what I am on this earth to do, and helped the people closest to me understand me better.

Figuring out what I value most (what I refer to as my "highest value") has caused such a great shift in my thinking. Until I did this I enjoyed my physio work and my role as a clinic owner, but I felt unsure about my bigger picture in life.

Interestingly, it is common for us to be able to spot another person's highest values much more easily than we can identify them in ourselves. When we are living to our highest values we are energised, inspired, and we generally don't require external motivation and managing to get us to do the things we need to do.

I will give you a very simple example. Take the late Steve Irwin. One of his highest values was clearly wildlife conservation – the way he spoke about wildlife, the energy he had, the time and money he spent on protecting wildlife, and the huge goals he had to protect large areas of land in North Queensland from development were all indicators of his highest values.

My highest value is positively influencing people. I do this daily through treating patients, mentoring my team, interacting with referrers and businesspeople in my community and posting on my Facebook pages – and I hope that I am positively influencing you as you read these words.

When I am acting according to my highest value I feel like time stands still, I am completely in the moment, I have huge amounts of energy, and I am inspired. Naturally this is a feeling that is worth replicating and trying to achieve as often as possible for as long as possible.

The founder of this concept is a mentor who has taught me so much about myself; he is an American behavioural expert by the name of Dr John Demartini. In my courses aimed at helping physios become leaders we go deeper into the topic of values, and personally this is the most valuable learning I have done in my career to date. It has given me direction, and the satisfaction that I am on the right path in life – the path I was meant to follow.

My courses "Be the Ultimate Physio" and "Train the Ultimate Physio" discuss this concept in much more depth, and I can honestly say that the exercises based around determining my values have been the most beneficial personal development exercises I have done.

DISCOVERING WHO YOU REALLY ARE

Do you know who you are? What a stupid question. Of course you do. You are a person who displays honesty, integrity and other such qualities – at least this is the response I hear most often. But does this really mean anything more than just lip service?

Let's see how you can find out more about yourself and others ...

PERSONALITY PROFILING

DISC profiling has helped me understand more about myself and my natural strengths and weaknesses, and has also helped me better understand my patients and my employees. I would like to credit Jason Smith, owner of the Back In Motion franchise group, for introducing me to the concept of DISC personality profiling during his Iceberg Leadership courses.

DISC profiling is a simple series of questions that determine whether a person is: a) introverted or extroverted; and b) people focused or task focused. Now many people say to me they are concerned that such a method could lead to "pigeon-holing" people and treating people all the same, but over the years and after conducting DISC profiles with hundreds of current and potential team members at my clinic, I have found that this profile gives me a fairly instant snapshot into unique elements of a person's personality, as well as their strengths and their fears.

I will now describe to you the four different DISC personality types:

- **D:** an extroverted, task-focused person. 'D's tend to consider themselves leaders and frequently end up in leadership positions. They are outspoken and tend to be people in society we perceive to be dominant. Their skills are leading and getting things done, their weaknesses are they can lack empathy and concern for others. To get the most out of a D just get out of their way. A D's greatest fear is being taken advantage of. If you are a D, you probably just want me to summarise this book in five pages so you can get started on the most important parts without delay.

- **I:** an extroverted, people-focused person. 'I' people are the life of the party, and tend to attract people as the centre of attention. They are great at connecting with people and telling stories, and they tend to also be great salespeople. It's all about people for the I personality. Their main weakness is they have difficulty finishing things they start. To get the most out of an I, make it all about them, but do not reject them openly as this is their greatest fear.

- **S:** an introverted, people-focused person. If you know an 'S', they tend to be a rock – very stable, reliable, predictable and routine in their lives. S personalities are great for listening professions such as physio. They may seem stand-offish, but they just want to get to know you better before opening up. To get the most out of them you need to give them stability, certainty, and allow them to establish a routine. Beware of changing things too quickly or too often, as this is their greatest fear.

- **C:** an introverted, task-focused person. 'C' personalities are detail-oriented people who are often great with words or numbers. Being introverted, they tend to take time to build relationships with people, but what they lack in verbal communication they more than make up for in thought – their brains go at 100 miles an hour. They tend to be exact, black-and-white sort of people. They are great at finishing tasks, as it's their strength, but god forbid they have to stand up and talk in front of a crowd. To get the most out of them, give them detail, rules, systems, structures and checklists. But be careful of criticising them – this is their greatest fear.

So these are the four personality profiles in the DISC profile. The best part of DISC profiling from my perspective is the simplicity. I also use DISC profiling for patients as I will generally tailor my communication with them based on a quick assessment of their DISC profile.

How should you use DISC profiling? Firstly, apply the DISC process to yourself and see what you think. Does the profile match elements of your personality? You could then also do a DISC profiling exercise with your partner and people close to you, as I have found it helps them to know more about themselves too.

However, DISC profiling's greatest value in my opinion is with your team and employees. It helps you to better understand your colleagues, and their strengths, weaknesses and preferred communication styles, which is invaluable in running a business. DISC profiling is another focus of The Ultimate Physio courses, and is particularly relevant for physio clinic owners, to get to know your team better, how they communicate, and what makes them tick.

THE IMPORTANCE OF BEING VULNERABLE

We physios can be a very guarded lot. We all want to be the best, the smartest, to fix the most patients, to have the most knowledge, the best hands-on skills, the most successful practice. Rarely are we prepared to be vulnerable and to say that someone is better than us at something, or admit we don't know the answer to something we really should know, or acknowledge that we may have forgotten something we learned years ago that we don't use in our daily practice and may not have needed to use for years.

I've learned a lesson about how to be happier every day in my physio career, and it has *nothing to do with physio*. It started to happen when I began to very honestly answer my patients' questions with three very scary words for a physio: "I don't know".

THE POWER OF SAYING 'I DON'T KNOW'

Now, for anyone in the health profession those three words are very hard to say. You would think as a patient they are also very hard words to hear, but I will tell you they are much easier words to hear than, "You're wrong", "It's all in your head", "You're just going to have to learn to live with it", and many other assertive comments that mask the fact that sometimes as health professionals we should be saying that we don't know.

When I started saying this to patients, what I initially felt was a dent to my pride. *How could I not know?* I have successfully treated thousands of patients with a huge variety of presentations, and some with very challenging problems.

But I've learned that if you tell a patient "I don't know", sometimes it can free you from your fear of giving them the wrong diagnosis, the wrong plan and the wrong advice. For many patients who ask me questions based on future outcomes regarding their condition, I will tell them I don't know exactly how their condition will play out, but based on their progress and with my intervention we can construct a really good plan to help them achieve their goals and live a life without pain, which we can modify as needed as time passes.

Many physios and business consultants in the physio space will tell you that you need a solid treatment plan with the patient committing to a block of treatment up front, but this block booking based on predictions has never really worked for me. I will still make sure my patient receives a high level of service, and I'm definitely not afraid of being accused of over-servicing as I do see my patients frequently and they get great results, but my predictive skills are not as good as some of these physios who block book, and I am not afraid to admit this. Yes, patients do want a plan, but in my experience the further into their treatment I can commit to timeframes the more accurate I can be.

But back to being vulnerable.

In my life as a physio I admit that I may not be the best physio in the world and there may be other physios who are better than me. Admitting this frees me from the shackles of needing to compete with every other physio around to be the best, which allows me to focus on myself and how I can improve as a physio, clinic owner and – most importantly – as a person, rather than constantly comparing myself to someone else who I may perceive as having better skills, communication or results than me.

So how can you start to be vulnerable in a safe environment? Start being vulnerable to yourself. If you don't know the answer to something, don't kid yourself that you do. Be brave enough to say to yourself, "I'm not sure", then go and research and find your best answer to the question asked. Once you are comfortable being honest and vulnerable with yourself, you can start to do so with others, including your patients. Be honest with people and they will detect how genuine you are, and you will feel more comfortable in your own skin. This is a really big step towards being happy.

PLAYING ABOVE THE BAR

I almost didn't write this chapter, but on reflection I feel it is my responsibility to you to do so, and I'm glad I did as this is a rule to live by if you want to succeed both as a physio and in life generally.

In life we all encounter problems, mistakes and challenges. As a clinic owner, leader of a team and a father, I encounter more of these than most. How we act and behave through difficult times is a mark of our true character.

ABOVE THE BAR

If you want to be a person of truly great character, who people trust and respect, then you must learn to live above the bar:

Ownership

Blame

Excuses

Denial

You will notice there is only one word above the bar: ownership.

OWNERSHIP

Let's start by considering what ownership actually is. We learn about this concept when we are young through our parents, or at school. As an adult in business it has a completely different meaning.

Ownership in my physio and clinic owner journey has continued to evolve over the years. At the heart of this concept I am responsible for everything that happens in my clinic and in my life, both good and bad. When our clinic doesn't have enough new clients, the problem is not "the economy". When my team are not happy, or not performing as well as I would like them to, it is not their fault. When my business's bottom line is not good enough, it is nobody's fault but mine.

That's ownership.

I have realised the benefit of truly owning my problems and challenges. To truly own a problem is to acknowledge it, which means being vulnerable. After acknowledging the problem, I can work through a solution, sometimes alone and sometimes with help.

Have you ever treated a patient who doesn't seem to be getting better as quickly as both you and she would like? The first step in taking ownership of your care of the patient is acknowledging to yourself and to her that you may need to do something different. What does this conversation look like? For starters, it's not an easy one, but I can assure you it is much better than if you keep rebooking her and one day she just doesn't turn up for her appointment, and you never see her again.

Some of the best physio–patient relationships I have formed over the years start with me treating someone, not getting great results, owning their treatment pathway, changing my approach, and then seeing results for them.

So start to own up to some of the challenges in your life. Not getting great results at work? Your responsibility. Your finances are not in order? Your responsibility. Not as fit as you want to be? Your responsibility. Career not where you want it to be? Up to you to change it – nobody's fault but yours.

BELOW THE BAR

Let's now discuss below the bar behaviour. Unfortunately many people are more familiar with this type of behaviour than ownership.

BLAME

We have all blamed someone for something before, me included. If a patient is not getting better, is it because he hasn't been doing his exercises?

Instead of blaming his lack of recovery on not doing exercises, how about mutually finding a way for him to enjoy or see the benefits of these exercises so that he actually does them? Or getting him into a gym so he has extra accountability rather than giving only home exercises?

Blame is rife in our society today. The worst thing is, frequently we don't lay blame on others, we blame circumstances – the economy, the job market, competitors, even the weather (as sometimes my clinic is quiet on rainy days). Blaming others or circumstances is a way for you to deflect your problems, mistakes and challenges, so you don't have to face them.

EXCUSES

Excuses – we all have them. Think of the last time you ran late to an appointment. Did you come up with a reason (also known as an excuse)? Too many red traffic lights, stuck behind a slow car, couldn't find a parking space? Those are all excuses. Our patients throw these at us on a daily basis as well, especially regarding their home exercise programmes.

How do I feel when someone throws an excuse at me? Often I just roll my eyes. Sometimes I smile and nod, but more often than not I challenge them on their excuse in an effort to help them see that they need to own their problem.

If someone is late to an appointment I would rather them simply apologise and say that they will not do it again, rather than hearing all of their so-called reasons.

When someone throws an excuse at you, they often start their sentence with the word "but". A concept I borrowed from Paul Wright is I have a "yeah, but" hammer in my consulting room. Every time I say the words "yeah, but", I give myself a whack on the head with this big inflatable hammer. People must think I'm crazy, but it stops you using the word "but" all the time.

Start to catch yourself using the word "but". When do you use it? Do you use it much? What are the situations in which you use it? You may be surprised. Reducing use of the word "but" in my vocabulary has helped me own more of my problems and solve them.

DENIAL

The most offensive of all below the bar behaviour is denial. No, denial is not a river in Egypt. (I just became a Dad, so I just threw my first Dad joke at you. I promise there won't be any more in the book.)

Denial is not only deflecting or excusing a problem or mistake, it's pretending it never happened. Denial is most applicable to mistakes, especially small ones. If you have a big problem in your life it is hard to pretend it doesn't exist. It's much easier to deny small problems.

Many people will deny out of fear – the fear that they may be punished due to a mistake or problem they have created. In my business this couldn't be further from the truth. In my business, when a mistake is made I need to know about it. Our team discusses the mistake, owns it, and as the clinic owner I own everyone's mistakes, and we learn from them.

Mistakes are how we learn. What I consider to be a negative element of school is that when we are learning, mistakes are considered to be bad. This social conditioning can often make us fearful of making mistakes. My Business Coach Brad Flynn has a great saying: "you win some, you learn some". I think of this saying every time I make a mistake, and believe me I make plenty, although I do my best to learn from them and to not make the same mistake repeatedly.

Do not fear making mistakes; they help you grow.

* * *

Owning your mistakes, problems and challenges frees you from them as you can work on them. If you blame, make excuses or deny, the problem or mistake can follow you around until you own it. So, be honest with yourself: where do you play life – above or below the bar?

I do my best to play above the bar, but I don't always do so (notice what I just said is an excuse – the statement began with my least favourite word!).

Exercise: Catch yourself when you say the word "but"

What is the context?

Are you making an excuse or justifying an action or behaviour?

Stop, and reframe the sentence.

Make sure you take ownership of the problem, challenge or mistake.

BE, DO, HAVE

In our physio careers – and in our lives – we all want to have something. That something can be success, happiness, money, status, recognition, love, credibility, or many other things.

I'm sure from time to time you have thought about what you want to have in life. A very common thing that almost all of us want to have here in Australia is the great Australian dream – your own home.

I need to pay credit to my business coach and good friend Brad Flynn from Actioncoach International for this whole chapter, as I have learned this concept from him, and it is one of the most valuable and applicable concepts I have learned in my life. Brad teaches that to get what you want in life, there is a simple formula you need to follow:

Be × Do = Have

So what you have in life is the result of multiplying what you do and who you are ("be").

What do I mean by this? Let's have a look.

'DO'

I'm going to assume that you know what the "do" component refers to – *doing stuff*. To address the "do" part of the equation briefly, I would like to discuss the two types of tasks that we do in life:

- urgent tasks

- important tasks.

Urgent tasks are things that need to be done now – answering the phone when it rings in your clinic, treating a patient at her scheduled appointment time, a team meeting, interacting with a person who comes into your clinic to make an appointment, and so on. These tasks are sometimes scheduled and sometimes unplanned, but regardless you need to do them as they are urgent.

The second type of task is the important task. Important tasks are things that you generally need to schedule or plan. Urgent tasks tend to trump important tasks, but important tasks are by nature … important. In a physio clinic, think marketing, complex case management, team mentoring, team building events, financial and statistical analysis, and so on.

Tasks will fall into one of four categories:

- **Non-important, non-urgent tasks.** Limit these trivial and wasteful tasks. This includes things like surfing Facebook or the internet for hours. Try to eliminate these tasks from your average day if you want to get more done, especially if you are spending hours rather than just minutes on these.

- **Urgent, non-important tasks.** Delegate these tasks and minimise your personal investment in them. These tasks you don't actually have to do, as long as you have someone to delegate them to, which you can do given they are not important to you but may be to someone else. Think of a task a physio doesn't like doing but an admin staff member may enjoy; such as completing the bulk of patient details in your paperwork.

- **Urgent, important tasks.** Manage these tasks according to necessity. If a patient, team member or key stakeholder in your clinic needs something done, do it in a timely manner, as soon as you are able. These tasks for a clinic owner include fighting fires in your clinic and dealing with minor crises. For instance, in 2014 while I was on holidays, my clinic flooded and my awesome team helped to limit the damage – this was the definition of an urgent, important task.

- **Non-urgent, important tasks.** These are generally planning tasks. The key with these tasks is to align them to your values and focus on your strategy.

My challenge to you is, when we spend the bulk of our time at work "doing", we gravitate more towards urgent rather than important tasks. Next time you are at work I would recommend considering whether you are spending your non-patient contact time in the most efficient way possible.

A good resource to help you establish if you are doing the right things at work is a spreadsheet called the "time audit". Credit for the time audit goes to my business coach, Brad Flynn from Actioncoach. The time audit helps you to list all of the tasks you do in a day, which you can then categorise into one of the four categories of urgency and importance as listed above.

You can find the Time Audit on the resources page at www.ultimatephysio.com.au.

'BE'

I hope you read some of the endorsements at the front of this book. These endorsements come from some of the true leaders of the physiotherapy profession, especially in private practice. If you read these endorsements carefully you will see that these giants of the physio profession haven't just focused on the "do", they have focused on the "be" element in their lives.

Looking back at my career as a physio and a clinic owner so far, I have made one big error that I'm going to enlighten you on, in the hope you don't make the same mistake.

The problem is, most physios and clinic owners I know make this error too. If you keep making this error you will most likely burn out, or look back at certain parts of your career with regret, having wished you took more risks, made more impact, did more of what you love, found your purpose, or worse still got out of the physio profession sooner!

What is this critical mistake?

Too much "do", not enough "be".

Going back to our model of Be × Do = Have, if your "do" score is one million and your "be" score is zero, you won't have what you want to have.

But how do you "be"?

To "be" you need to grow as a person. You need to learn about who you really are and what drives and motivates you. You need to understand your strengths and weaknesses. You need to find your true purpose, and live a life of significance, happiness, and being present in the moment as much as you possibly can.

In the past five years I have learned more about myself than in the 30 years prior. How have I done this? Leadership, management, and personal development education. The significant amount of work I have done on my "be" has led to me now teaching these concepts to physios and clinic owners, as I have observed that our traditional educational model has left us – as well as other medical and allied health professionals – severely lacking in this area.

I believe there is a direct relationship between the higher and more specific our technical knowledge ("do"), and the challenges we face in learning and accepting new concepts and learnings that challenge our existing beliefs ("be").

I read at least one book on business or personal development a week. I listen to audiobooks in my car on the way to and from work. I do a nice blend of physio, business and personal development courses – generally five to six major courses a year. I have mentors who help me with business, physio, personal development, and I even have a head coach (my psychologist).

Now I'm not suggesting you must go the whole hog, but at least consider which of these options for personal growth fits with who you are, your lifestyle, and what you want out of life.

But I urge you, find out what your true purpose is, before your life passes you by.

PHYSIO

WHY WE NEED TO REDEFINE WHAT WE DO

HOW SHOULD WE DEFINE PHYSIOTHERAPY?

So what actually is physiotherapy? When I check the Google keyword search there are literally millions of people all over the world asking this question. I think this is actually sad for us; I mean, they don't type in "what is a doctor", "what is a dentist", or "what is a pharmacist".

How does the Australian Physiotherapy Association define physiotherapy?

It states that:

Physiotherapy is a healthcare profession that assesses, diagnoses, treats, and works to prevent disease and disability through physical means. Physiotherapists are experts in movement and function who work in partnership with their patients, assisting them to overcome movement disorders, which may have been present from birth, acquired through accident or injury, or are the result of ageing or life-changing events.[2]

I do not believe that this definition is simple or concise enough. How does a potential patient understand the statement above? What are "physical means"? Does a complicated, lengthy definition of what we do impress people who might need our services? I don't think so.

Let's have a look at Google. When I type "what is physiotherapy" into Google's search engine I get the following definition:

Physiotherapy is the treatment of disease, injury, or deformity by physical methods such as massage, heat treatment, and exercise rather than by drugs or surgery.

Wow! Massage and heat packs! I studied at university for years to be a physio to treat my patients with massage and heat packs ... did you? This sounds like a massage therapist's job.

So let's recap. The APA uses a wordy definition that means little to our patients (who are the reason we are in private practice) and Google says we are glorified massage therapists. And as the saying goes, you are who Google says you are.

The truth is that not as many people in Australia know what physio is and who it can help as they should. Why is this? Because collectively *we cannot define what we do as a profession* – and this is a big problem! We are not getting the message across. And if *we* can't figure it out, how can the people who need us?

Let's contrast this with the chiropractic profession. The chiropractic profession started with the remarkable situation where you did not need a qualification to be a chiropractor. You could just hang a sign outside your clinic door saying you were a chiropractor, and that was enough. The chiropractic profession has not embraced

---

2   APA website, 2017.

evidence-based practice as much as the physiotherapy profession, and yet patients flock to them in droves!

I consider that the chiropractic profession has defined what it does very well, and the patients and potential patients understand this. If you feel your back has "gone out" (where it has gone to I'm not sure) or your spine is out of alignment, or your hips are out, you go to the chiropractor to have it all realigned. It feels okay for a while, and then over time the pain creeps back, and another visit to the chiro gets you feeling good again.

While as physios we may criticise this model, the chiropractic profession has clearly defined what it does, how it does it, who it can help, and a general treatment model that most chiropractors use, which is intensive initial treatment followed by less frequent reviews.

PHYSIO AS A FIRST-CONTACT PAIN EXPERT

As part of my vision, a physio needs to be seen within the community as a pain expert – a first-contact practitioner for people who are in pain, to assist them in differentially diagnosing the source of their pain, eliminating medical factors, understanding how their routines and habits contribute to their pain, and helping them achieve pain-free status.

Here are some of the treatments patients can receive when they see a physio: heat, cold, TENS, interferential, massage, trigger point therapy, dry needling, muscle energy techniques, neurodynamic therapy, Maitland, McKenzie or Mulligan therapy, craniosacral therapy, PNF stretching, traditional stretching, pilates, stability/motor control exercises, gym-based strength training, mobilisation, manipulation, pain education, ergonomic advice, cognitive functional therapy, worksite assessment, gym training programme, hydrotherapy, Ridgway Method, back rehab programmes, neurological rehab, balance rehab – and I could go on.

But none of these terms will mean anything to the people who need us. So, it's our job to come up with a description of what we do that they can relate to and that is meaningful to them, and so that they will understand when and why they should come to see us. When we define our profession we need to define it from our patients' perspectives. If we do not do this we risk the indignity of being left behind by the people who are most important in our profession – the patients we are meant to be helping.

Here is my preferred definition of a physio:

A physio is a pain and movement expert. Your physio will find out why you are in pain, help you get rid of your pain as quickly as possible, get you moving again, and get you back to doing the things you enjoy.

My preferred definition is a big-picture definition. It is patient-centric. It does not include any aspect of how we treat a patient, which most patients aren't that concerned with anyway (they just want to get out of pain and get back to living life).

The reason I define physio as I have is this: if a patient knows and understands what physios do and what we can help her with, she will come to see us for advice. That horribly low proportion of people who use physios as first-contact practitioners for pain and injury, which a mentor of mine said was in the realm of 2.6% back in 2009, will become 5%, then 10%, then 20%, and the possibilities are endless.

But we can only achieve this with a change of mindset.

A physio is the best person to see if you have pain and if you have seen your doctor who has run you through all sorts of tests to make sure your problem is not life threatening, and you don't know what to do next. So let's start to spread the word!

CHAPTER

6

THE RESURGENCE OF THE MANUAL THERAPIST

GETTING HANDS-ON

University physiotherapy training in Australia is cutting edge and world class. But the challenge with university training for an intuitive-type degree such as physio is that we are practising manual techniques on each other, and most of us when we're at uni are healthy and fit with no significant pain or injuries. From my perspective this challenged me regarding my development of skills based around assessing patients with real problems going on in their bodies.

I remember treating my first patient in my prac year. I had no idea what to do. I had never had an opportunity to speak to anyone having any symptoms of pain or movement dysfunction, as in our second and third clinical years at the University of Queensland we had practised on other physiotherapy students. We would palpate muscles, mobilise joints, test active and passive movement all over the body, and not really know what we should be looking for or feeling for.

It is actually quite challenging as a young practitioner getting a feel for what might be wrong in a person's body when we are testing other young and healthy people in a clinical prac setting. However, due to practicality this seems to be the most logical way to give us some initial hands-on experience.

In recent times one of the more amazing phenomena in the allied health world is the seemingly endless overlap between professions: physios, chiropractors, osteopaths, myopractors, exercise physiologists, Bowen therapists and so on. We are all becoming more like each other. Much of the overlap in these allied health professions (barring exercise physiology) is the use of manual therapy. So how is physio any different from chiropractic or osteopathy from a manual therapy perspective? As physios we need to develop superior manual therapy skills when assessing and treating compared to these other professions. I believe we can develop this superior skillset in the area of manual assessment.

One area of physiotherapy study in which it is near impossible to gain good practical experience is in palpating pathological tissue versus normal tissue. Upon graduating I had no confidence in my ability to find a problem in a person's body. Therefore instead of doing a really solid clinical physical assessment upon my graduation, I would rely on some of the recipe-based treatments for certain body parts.

For lower back pain we would teach transversus exercises and show the person a stretch where he pulled one knee up to his shoulder. For neck pain we would teach deep neck flexor strengthening exercises. For knee pain we would give inner range quads exercises. For shoulder pain we would give scapular stabilising exercises followed by rotator cuff strengthening exercises. For acute ankle sprains we would use the RICE principle and then teach balance and proprioceptive exercises.

In the modern clinical setting, I find that plenty of GPs I know are referring patients in pain to exercise physiologists (EPs) purely for exercise prescription. The EPs are quite good at teaching these exercises. In my opinion we do not want to be competing with EPs. Why would we compete when we have the potential to learn one of the most remarkable skills a person can have: to be able to facilitate pain-free movement with your hands?

I consider my palpation and manual skills to be the absolute cornerstone of my job. Sadly I feel that this is the skill I find is most lacking in physios throughout Australia. A lack of manual therapy confidence, and not necessarily a lack of skills, can make us revert to less effective methods, including electrotherapy and generic exercise sheets detailing many different stretches that are non-specific to the patient's condition. From my experience and after asking hundreds of patients for feedback, this "fall back" treatment is damaging to our profession, reduces our credibility, and worst of all, leaves our patients feeling dissatisfied. After all, they are paying good money to see a pain and movement expert.

MY INSIDER'S TRICK TO PALPATING A HYPERTONIC MUSCLE

I love palpating around a patient's body, probing for areas of hypertonicity, palpable tenderness and dysfunction. This adds significantly to my clinical reasoning process, and helps me give the patient the best diagnosis possible. A diagnosis is important to the patient so she can understand what is wrong in her body. I will teach you my insider's trick to palpating a hypertonic muscle.

A healthy muscle feels like a raw steak. You can move it around under your fingers, and the patient does not twitch or react in pain when you palpate it. A sore muscle often feels like an overcooked steak. It is ropey, hard, and can sometimes even feel like you are palpating a bone. If you find a muscle like this it does not mean that you have found the patient's problem, but it is definitely a sign that this muscle is not 100%, and it adds to your overall clinical picture and understanding of your patient's problem.

When you are palpating a joint you should be feeling for reactivity, range of movement and end feel. If the joint is sore to palpate, as well as if it does not move well on either a PPIVM or a PAIVM (different types of joint glides), it can be a sign that this joint is moving dysfunctionally, and again adds to the clinical picture.

I have learned that you get no results from treating muscles or joints that are not initially tender to touch, or that do not feel stiff to palpate. If a joint is non-tender and not hypomobile there is no reason to mobilise it. So get cracking. Your job is to feel as many normal and symptomatic muscles and joints as possible. I estimate that it took me the first five years of my career to gain confidence with palpation, and to learn to trust my hands and what I felt when I placed my hands on my patient.

Prominent author and thinker Malcolm Gladwell wrote in his book *Outliers* that he considered it took 10,000 hours to master a particular skill to a high level of proficiency. I estimate that for the first 10 years of my career I did 40 clinical hours per week, half of which I had my hands on my patients. So, 20 hours per week. And let's assume I had a really busy year and worked the equivalent of 50 weeks – after all, this is private practice; you had better get used to working hard! So in one year I would have clocked up 1,000 hours of palpation. So coming into my tenth year as a physio I had clocked up my 10,000 hours of proficiency. I am now in my fourteenth year of my physio career.

So don't worry or despair if after one or two years you are still not confident with your palpation. I sure wasn't. Just keep persisting, thinking, trusting your skills, building up your repertoire, and make sure you get to that 10-year mark.

If you are a student, a good idea is to approach your local physio clinic and offer to do some massage for them. Help your friends and family out by doing massages for as many people as you can find. Buy yourself a $50 fold-up massage table secondhand off eBay and you will suddenly be the most popular physio student in the neighbourhood.

My final thought on this topic is that I am becoming increasingly aware of a large number of physios within our profession who are feeling increasingly uneasy, even guilty, for performing manual therapy as part of a consultation. I believe evidence-based practice is responsible for this, as randomised controlled trials do not "support the use of manual therapy" in physio consultations, although I have seen some RCTs which discuss the use of manual plus exercise therapy as being of more clinical benefit than either manual therapy or exercise therapy delivered on their own.

Having now treated more than 8,000 patients over the last 13 years, I rely more on my clinical judgment than on research within a consultation. It's really hard to take it when people dish out constant criticism of manual therapy when you treat someone with a movement dysfunction, apply a manual intervention, and their movement dysfunction disappears after the intervention. I will then teach an exercise that achieves as similar a result as possible as my manual technique does. The immediate improvement the patient receives from the manual therapy gets them onside so they become more compliant with their therapy and get better outcomes. If you have ever seen Brian Mulligan or Michael Ridgway perform live treatment on clients then you will understand what I'm talking about.

In my opinion, a physio skilled at both manual therapy and exercise prescription beats a physio skilled at only exercise prescription any day of the week.

And what do our patients want? They want us to touch them. A regular criticism I hear from a patient who visits a GP or specialist is "they didn't even touch me". We need to gain our patients' confidence and trust through fulfilling their expectations, which involves at least a physical assessment.

CHAPTER

7

SYSTEMATISING YOUR PHYSIO EXPERIENCE

In business we are told all about the many benefits of having systems, procedures and processes. Systems allow for consistency of delivery, so that different members of your work team can follow a structure for a particular task they need to perform in order to get the best outcome and ensure the greatest chance of success, provided the system is set up properly.

THE GOLDEN ARCHES

The best example of a business that has systems that operate smoothly is everyone's favourite family restaurant, McDonald's. McDonald's systems are so good they can employ 15-year-old staff and 18-year-old managers to run the place, without an adult in sight. In a place like McDonald's everything appears to run quite smoothly from the customer's perspective, and on my rare visits there I am always amazed by the initiative shown by such young people.

The way in which McDonald's prospers is in having an environment that is highly systematised – if one person doesn't follow the system they are the odd one out, and they are either pulled back into line or cast aside.

CAN WE SYSTEMISE PHYSIOTHERAPY?

Systematising physiotherapy is an interesting topic. One can argue that given how many different presentations we see in our clients and the fact that no two people's pain profiles are the same, it's impossible to systematise a consultation. But I beg to differ.

I believe we can systematise how we deliver a consultation to help us achieve a certain amount of consistency across and between our consultations, to help eliminate missing things we all regret missing during a consultation, to give the patient the best results, but also to keep us fresh so we don't burn excessive energy during a consultation. I have seen the results of this in some therapists I have worked with, and long term this feeling can result in burnout. My philosophy in my consultations is to always leave something in reserve in terms of energy levels, as we deserve to live our lives too and we need some energy left to do this.

WHAT DOES MY CONSULTATION PROCESS LOOK LIKE?

It was only recently that I had my eyes opened to the best way to articulate the massive value that physiotherapists provide for our patients, and from this I have created a system in my practice for how I treat people. This system revolves around a thought process for how to structure a consultation, in terms of how you choose your assessment, treatment and recommendations. This is a system within a system: my Pain Transformation Blueprint™, which I will take you through now. This is an example of a system you can use in a physiotherapy business.

Step 1: The interview

1   Thorough history of the patient's current and previous injuries

2   Detailed health assessment

3   Daily habits analysis

Step 2: Physical testing

1   Posture analysis

2   Movement analysis

3   Special testing

4   Palpation (hands-on) assessment

Step 3: Diagnosis

1   Understanding the problem

2   Explaining the problem to the patient

Step 4: Treatment

1   Hands-on treatment

2   Pain relief

3   Improved body movement

Step 5: Recommendations

1   Patient education

2   Exercises

3   Stretches

Step 6: Plan

1   Patient recovery plan

2   Joint implementation

3   Review progress

Essentially this outlines everything I do in a physio consultation, but packaged in a way that clearly explains to my patients the huge value and numerous steps that occur during a process that to them seems quite seamless.

Notice how I have simplified this system and translated it into "patient speak". Once I began articulating my consultation in this way, it produced the mind shift I needed to value what I provide in the consultation even more. When you look at the above outline it articulates each step in the consultation process clearly, in a way the patient can understand.

When people ask the question, "What happens in a physio consultation?", an explanation of this process gives them both clarity and reinforces my authority and expertise. I'm not just getting straight into the treatment, which many physios are guilty of, and this systematised process allows me not to have to think too much regarding how I structure my consultation, but just to follow the process.

The caveat is that this process needs to be refined, tested and measured, and improved over thousands of consultations by you, the practitioner. I have always maintained that I do not want to tell other physios what to do, but to give explanations of what works and doesn't work for me. This is called Gestalt learning, and is the best way to teach.

PROCESS-DRIVEN THINKING IN A CONSULTATION

I will often say to young physios I'm mentoring that I don't want to teach you what to do, I want to teach you how to think. With this philosophy in mind I have developed a simple system which I have had new grad physios implement, and this has produced great results in terms of organising their thinking before and within a consultation.

Do you sometimes wish that you could just have your consultation process and structure on autopilot so you didn't have to think about every little thing you have to do in a consultation and just focus on your patient? Especially as a young physio? With a bit of preparation, this may just be possible.

Let me introduce you to the Consultation Planning Quadrant™ (CPQ).

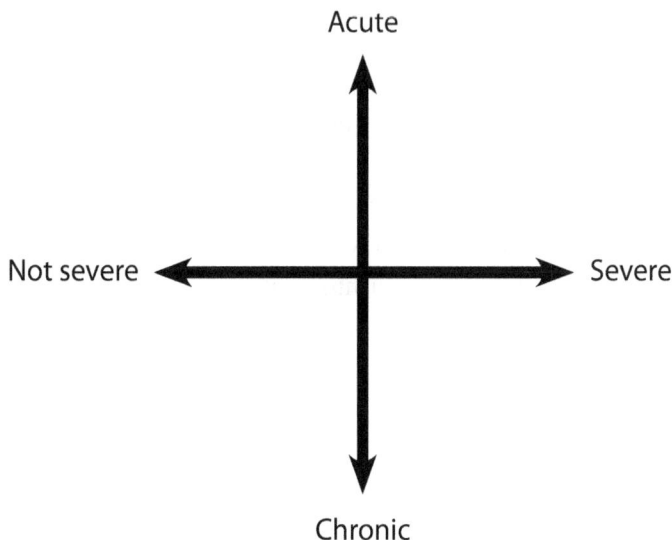

What the CPQ describes is a method for determining which assessment, treatment and recommendations you will implement based on two different scales:

- the severity of a person's pain

- the length of time they have had their condition.

In my experience these two variables guide me as to the simplest way (and we need to keep this simple) to determine which assessment techniques I will use.

A simple example is this: a patient who has a lifting injury of his back from work comes into your clinic and can hardly move. When assessing him you don't want to do anything like repetitive movements of his lumbar spine which could significantly exacerbate his issue, nor will he want to lie in prone position, nor will your recommendations include high-level functional exercises.

To get the best use out of the CPQ you need one of these documents for each body area, but let's just start with back, neck, hip, shoulder and knee as these are the most common areas of pain.

The next step is to complete the four quadrants based on the assessment, treatment and recommendations for people with pain ranging from mild to severe, and for length of pain presentation ranging from acute to chronic. If you can have one of these quadrants for each common body area you will be able to quickly reference your toolkit and determine which assessment and treatment techniques to apply for a patient with pain ranging from mild to severe, and for people with conditions ranging from acute to chronic.

This quadrant is actually most effective when determining which methods to *leave out* of an assessment or treatment; for example, avoiding repetitive movements on a patient with acute, severe discogenic back pain who limps into your clinic and can hardly move. For young physios the Consultation Planning Quadrant removes risk, which is a positive step for the confidence of a young therapist.

For a blank template of the Consultation Planning Quadrant, check out our resources at www.ultimatephysio.com.au.

Exercise: A practice consultation

Perform a regular physio consultation on someone you know.

Do everything you would normally do for a paying customer.

At the end of the consultation, ask your patient/friend to describe to you in their language everything you did in the consultation, from start to finish.

Does their description of what your consultation looks like match the service that you intend to provide?

Was there anything missing, or anything they didn't completely understand? Ask them.

When you have written down the points they describe in your consultation process, start to refine it.

What else do you need to add? Can you take away elements that are unimportant to save time or reduce confusion?

The best way to determine your success and clarity in your consultation process is how clearly your patients can describe how you helped them. For example:

> "My physio sat down with me and asked lots of questions to try to understand what caused my problem, not just where my pain is. He then did lots of different movements of my body, and put his hands on me to feel the muscles in the sore area. To help, he did some hands-on physio techniques to loosen up the muscles, he taught me how to start to get the muscles loose by exercising them, and he gave me some advice about how to stop the problem getting worse. At the end he told me when to come back and what we will do next session. I now feel relieved that someone can help me get rid of my pain."

CHAPTER

8

MAKING EXERCISE PRESCRIPTION FUN

WHY DO WE PRESCRIBE EXERCISES?

So as physios, why do we prescribe exercises? I have two reasons for doing this myself:

- to give my patients a way to fix themselves, both now and in the future

- to help them get better quicker.

Let's have a look at these.

ALLOWING PATIENTS TO FIX THEMSELVES

The first reason is the obvious reason: helping the patient cope actively with his problem, increasing his self-efficacy and ability to fix his own pain, and promoting positive beliefs about his condition or pain and the fact that he controls it and not having it control him.

Prescribing exercise is what our profession teaches us, but it's not what the bulk of our patients want, based on my experience and questioning of thousands of patients over the years. Many people are inherently lazy – they are hoping for a quick fix, and want to get better without having to do anything themselves. Some of them want a magic wand. Our job is to train them to want to do the exercises.

SPEEDING UP RECOVERY TIME

The second reason – to speed up recovery time – is more interesting to me as I believe it's the next level of thinking from the first reason. In this chapter I will explain why, and how to achieve this in your consultation. This is also what our patients are crying out for, and we must give it to them.

PERSONALISING THE EXERCISE REGIME

When I started my career there were these things called PEP pads. I think they stood for "personalised exercise prescription". Trouble is, they weren't particularly personalised! They were generic sheets of 10 or 12 exercises for specific body parts – one for the lumbar spine, neck, shoulder, and so on.

At the end of the consultation I would hand them to the patient and say, "Do these exercises". When she came back I found that she hadn't done them, and her condition was the same as when she was at their previous appointment. Her level of compliance reduced, and the trust relationship I was trying to build with her was compromised. She didn't believe in the process I was taking her through.

I became dissatisfied with these results, so I started to do what I was taught at university.

At university we were taught that transversus abdominis and deep neck flexor exercises fixed basically any spinal pain, as this was what research determined at the time – but this was not what I was seeing in practice. I would teach the exercises I had been told to teach. But patients had trouble with these exercises, which required a high degree of body awareness, and if you do them just slightly incorrectly you get no results, or make your condition worse. To me these seemed like too much of a cure-all philosophy – why should we prescribe them for almost any condition?

This is part of the challenge of being a new grad physio with too few tools in your toolkit – like being in one of those Roman Colosseum battles armed with just a stick.

DETERMINING WHICH EXERCISES WILL WORK BEST

The feedback I have received from young physios is that it's really hard to determine which exercises will work best so that they would have the confidence to prescribe only one or two exercises, rather than having to prescribe five or six exercises to get a good result. Here's my system for how to prescribe an exercise:

1   conduct a good assessment

2   develop a diagnosis

3   deliver some manual therapy that either reduces pain or improves movement

4   prescribe an exercise that mimics the result of the manual therapy.

For example, if trigger point release of the gluteus medius muscle helps the person move better, give him an exercise that makes the gluteus medius contract and relax and increases bloodflow to this muscle. My recipe for prescribing exercises, initially in the early phase of treatment when you are working to gain the patient's confidence with quick results, really is this simple.

I threw those exercise pads in the bin, and wondered why they were forced on us with such insistence. I thought there had to be more out there in terms of exercise prescription. I had determined that giving too many non-specific exercises and prescribing the blanket exercises I had been taught at university were not yielding the results for my patients that I was hoping for. My thought process led me to the question of how do you determine which exercises work best for patients with certain conditions?

This got me thinking.

The first stage in the exercise prescription process I refined was giving exercises that were based entirely on positive findings from the person's examination and not just giving an exercise for the sake of it.

An example is, if the person's TA muscle (given this book is targeted to physios, this is what physios call the transversus abdominis muscle) does not test weak, I do not give a TA strength exercise. If the hamstring is not tight, I do not give a hamstring stretch. If the person has good posture, I do not give a posture exercise. I started to strip the process down and prescribe three exercises for each patient. Patient compliance improved. The exercises took less time, patients were more willing to do them, and their results improved.

With the passing of years and seeing better results with this process I now give the absolute minimum number of different exercises per session – at least early on in the process – to get the patient fixed faster.

One of my favourite books is *The One Thing* by Gary Keller. The premise of the book is that you achieve better results if you focus on one thing. This one thing however must be the most important thing to get the best results. As my assessments improved I learned which exercises produced better results. The better the results between sessions, the more the patients wanted to come back and get fixed more quickly.

EXERCISE PROGRESSION

The next step in the process for me was making sure I appropriately progressed the patient's exercises. I found that a big mistake I was making was relying on patients doing the exercises I prescribed correctly, but 9 out of 10 times I observed that they actually weren't. This made me implement a protocol to check how they were doing the previous exercise at the start of each session. Patients liked this approach – it reinforced the importance of the exercise in their eyes, and removed confusion. Instantly they had a more relaxed and focused approach to the exercise.

I am quite flexible with all of these parameters, as I base the correct dosage on being enough to produce results but not so much as to irritate the problem. I believe that patients need a certain dosage of exercise to improve their condition and a different and often lesser dose to maintain their condition, although in saying this the difficulty of the exercises needs to be progressed for them to still see results through their journey, and must mimic the movements that at any stage influence or provoke their symptoms.

A simple example here is a patient who has knee pain running who has a weak calf and gluteus medius muscle. I will initially help her strengthen these muscles, but a mistake I regularly see is a patient will be doing double calf raises to strengthen her calves but will not be progressed onto a single calf raise exercise that mimics the action of running.

I have also discovered the difference between prescribing stretches and strengthening (or muscle activation, as I call them) exercises. My conclusion here is that stretches have a benefit for gaining mobility early on but the results are temporary, while strengthening exercises seem to produce greater benefit early on and the results are more consistent and last longer – but only if you strengthen something that is weak, and not already strong.

An example is good old tennis elbow. My philosophy here is that the common extensor origin where the pain seems to sit is not an area that is weak, but too strong. The wrist extensors do loads of work in people who grip, type, lift, and so on. I have found that for these patients, strengthening bicep, supinator, rotator cuff and periscapular muscles produces fast and lasting results, as opposed to good old wrist extensor strengthening exercises. Of course this is not the case in all presentations of tennis elbow, but with a good enough assessment and finding weakness in some of those muscles I mentioned the results can come quickly.

* * *

So to summarise my philosophy on exercises as a therapist who predominantly enjoys the manual therapy and communication sides of the consultation more than exercise prescription, I had to devise a method that made teaching exercises exciting and fun for me, as when I feel this way I transfer my energy to my patients who are then inspired and do their exercises.

My fun game I now play with exercises revolves around the question, "How can I get my patients fixed as quickly as possible, giving them the minimum amount of exercise that they are willing to do?" Obviously this is a different amount for every person, from the elite athlete to the little old lady. When you get to know each patient's beliefs, fears and expectations from physio well enough you can make a judgment about this.

EXERCISE PRESCRIPTION FLOWCHART

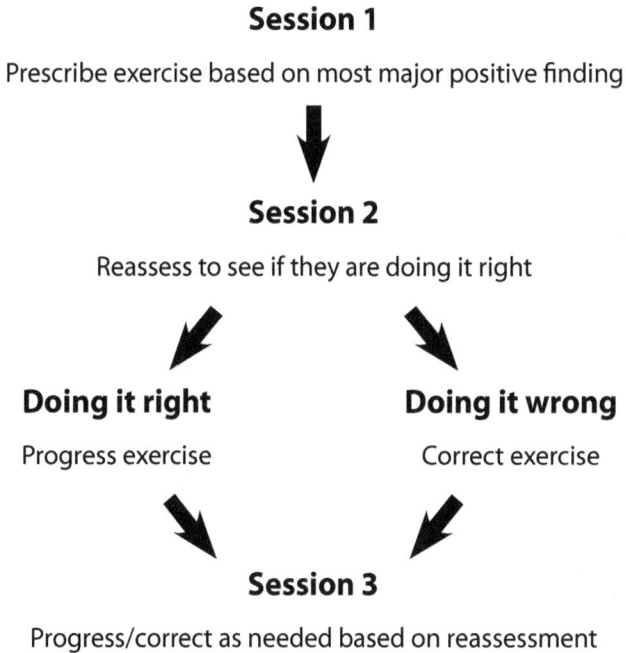

Session 1

Prescribe exercise based on most major positive finding

Session 2

Reassess to see if they are doing it right

Doing it right

Progress exercise

Doing it wrong

Correct exercise

Session 3

Progress/correct as needed based on reassessment

MANUAL THERAPY PLUS EXERCISES EQUALS BEST OUTCOMES

There is much conflicting research that attempts to determine whether manual therapy, exercise therapy, or a combination of both produces the best clinical outcomes. Depending on the patient's pathology or presenting symptoms, the outcomes of the various studies I have perused are vastly different.

I will give you my opinion about why manual therapy and exercise therapy combined produces the best clinical outcomes, and why this should be your method when treating a patient.

MANUAL THERAPY ONLY

First, let's consider how one type of therapy without the other produces a suboptimal outcome. Consider a patient in pain. He has soreness to sit, stand, walk, move, or can even have pain at rest. His pain can be constant, intermittent, severe, annoying, and even debilitating. So where do we start? How do we treat this patient?

If we assess our patient who is suffering from severe pain and find that he has point tenderness in his lower back and hip muscles, or tenderness to palpate over a facet joint, these are physical signs (I refer to them as "asterisk signs", courtesy of Michael Ridgway who taught me this terminology) rather than a diagnosis. To elicit a change in the resting tone of the muscle, I might perform a trigger point release on the muscle or a passive mobilisation technique in the joint. As well as a change in tone and joint mobility, this also provides afferentation, or input, to the dorsal horn of the spinal cord at a certain level.

Afferentation can be helpful to settle down a patient's pain levels, so we can apply some manual therapy to settle down his pain. If we apply this manual therapy, how long do you think the positive effect of this treatment will last? Hopefully long enough for the patient to feel some benefit from the treatment, to get up off the bed with a smile, and feel like his ability to move and bend has improved. But in my experience, people with more severe or chronic pain will not have a long-lasting effect due to problems with the way they move. If they keep moving the way they did before you started the treatment, the tissues will endure similar strain and the pain will return, in a matter of minutes to hours after the effect of the treatment has worn off.

EXERCISE THERAPY ONLY

So let's consider the alternative, which is exercise therapy. You have a patient with lower back pain who has a weak core. The person obviously needs to learn some transversus abdominis stabilisation exercises to improve her core strength. This person still has some impaired movement patterns due to her weak core.

My opinion is that if you simply teach the person transversus exercises you have not delved deeply enough into diagnosing why she is actually in pain. People who are in pain who do not first have their pain addressed with some form of manual therapy to help them move with less pain seem to be less confident in the outcome of their exercises, especially if the exercise does not produce an immediate improvement either in their pain levels or their ability to move. The patient has trouble understanding how this simple little exercise can change their severe pain. If the patient has doubts, their compliance can also be limited.

COMBINING THE TWO

People will always tell you they are going to do their home exercises three times a day, but if you have not gained their confidence by achieving some great initial results in relieving their pain then how much faith will they have in the advice you are giving them? Not as much faith as they would have had if you had given them some pain relief initially with some expert manual therapy, and then followed it up with the exercise to solidify the gains reached through treatment.

This is how I explain my regimen of treatment to my patients. During the treatment phase of the consultation we need to perform some high-quality, specific and targeted manual therapy to reduce their pain and help them to move better, and then consolidate the results of the manual therapy with an exercise to help the patient manage their symptoms, improve their strength, settle down their pain nerves, or move better.

HOW MANY EXERCISES SHOULD I PRESCRIBE?

Another one of my philosophies regarding exercises is that I generally will only give my patients one or two exercises in a physio session. My rationale is this: if I give my patients one or two exercises they will understand them if I explain them well, they are more likely to be compliant, they are more likely to achieve better results between treatments, and I am more likely to understand their condition as when they return I will run through my physical assessment with them to re-examine their asterisk signs to see if their physical signs have changed. This improves my understanding of their condition.

The alternative to this approach is the good old exercise sheet, with 10 different exercises on it. Traditionally physios tick the exercises to be done, write down the number of repetitions and the frequency with which the physio wants the patient to do the exercises, do not have time to demonstrate all of the exercises to see if the patient is doing them properly, and the patient leaves the consult not knowing which exercises are the most important, and not having the time or the focus to do all of these exercises at home.

The patient will generally return for the next consult feeling slightly embarrassed and guilty for not having done all the exercises, and feeling like she has failed in her homework. I do not believe the patient has failed us; I believe we have failed the patient. How many people enjoyed doing homework at school? How likely are our patients to do all of their assigned homework? Should we as their supportive therapists be making things specific and easy for them, or general and hard?

I find that 9 out of 10 people are doing their exercises incorrectly and with poor form. At the patient's second consultation I generally have to check to see if she is doing the exercise correctly, and make some minor changes to her technique to make sure she is getting the maximum result from the assigned exercise. If the patient is not doing the exercise correctly she is either not getting any benefit from the exercise or she could actually be making her symptoms worse.

When discussing this issue with patients I do not lay any blame. After all, they are not the physio, and they did not spend four years at university learning how to do exercises correctly. As physios who prescribe exercises to members of the public we cannot expect them to do our exercises correctly. I tell my patients that exercises are like Chinese Whispers – every day they do their exercises, the exercises change a little bit! Let's be a bit proactive in our exercise prescription, be responsible, assume our patients are doing their exercises incorrectly, and be thorough and clear when teaching our patients these exercises in the first place. Err on the side of giving them too little to do rather than too much to do.

My summary is that manual and exercise therapy together is great! Practise your manual therapy and palpation as much as possible to get a feel for what's normal and what isn't, and when teaching exercises be clear, specific, don't prescribe too many, and make sure you check with your patients at their next consultation as to whether they are doing their exercises correctly.

SELLING YOURSELF TO REFERRERS

I have a concern with the big picture of exercise prescription. Exercise physiology is quite a progressive profession, and they are currently aggressively marketing their profession to GPs as the experts when it comes to exercise prescription. I can tell you one area where physios have it all over exercise physiologists: prescribing exercises that give the patient quicker and longer lasting results without flaring up their pain. Our more advanced assessment skills give us a higher level ability to prescribe the right exercises based on individual patient needs and positive assessment findings. This is a difficult thing to explain to a GP, and I don't believe our profession has yet recognised this distinction. When more physios catch on to this we need to shout it from the rooftops. Do anything possible to let GPs know this is the case. I have found the best way to prove this for GPs or other potential referrers is to help them with their problem or help their spouse, parent or child.

As physios we are the best profession when it comes to exercise prescription that achieves the best outcomes for our patients, but we must get better at explaining why this is the case. Unfortunately for some of you less-business-minded physios who love to hide your value, the only way to overcome this is to learn to market yourself. I will teach you how to do this later in the book.

CHAPTER
9

NERVES: THE ROOT OF ALL PAIN

TESTING NEURAL TISSUE SENSITIVITY

If I could describe the most revolutionary moment in my clinical career to date, I can say without a doubt that it was the day I learned how to assess and treat neural tissue mechanosensitivity, or neural tension as it used to be known. We learned how to assess neural tension at uni but I didn't really understand when we should use these tests, what they told us, and why we should do them.

I did a course called Spinal level 1, and one of the instructors on that course gave us a taste of the practical side of neural tissue testing. After that course I thought, *wow, that was incredible – I have never seen anything like that before.* I wondered what type of patients this type of assessment and treatment was helpful for.

When I started doing professional development with Michael Ridgway at Baroona Physio in Milton, Brisbane, he elaborated on testing and treatment of neural tissue. Michael assesses the neural tissue sensitivity of every patient who walks through his door.

He finds that he gets the best outcomes if he can find signs of positive neural tissue sensitivity and reduce this neural tissue sensitivity before moving on to treating the muscles and joints.

As a young physio there were plenty of patients I would treat and I would be unsure as to how they would respond to my treatment. Some people would get better, some people's symptoms would stay the same, and some people's symptoms would "flare up" after the treatment. This got me thinking.

When my patient improved my treatment had either helped them or they were getting better on their own anyway. Sometimes I could understand how the treatment that I applied had helped them, and sometimes I couldn't explain how I had helped them. Regarding my patients whose symptoms stayed the same, I felt that I had simply not treated the right area of their body to produce positive results. I had not really found their problem.

The patients who flared up with treatment I was really worried about, but I shouldn't have been. I now know that I had found an area I could treat and that could produce improvement in their symptoms, but either the area I had treated was neurally sensitive, was stabilising the body segment and I had released a muscle that was primarily holding that segment together, or had just been in this state for a long while and flared up due to sudden input.

The concept of sensitivity of the nervous system made sense. When a patient came in and said, "I was really sore after your treatment", there had to be a reason for this, as traditionally I was quite gentle with my manual therapy, which I consider to be the best approach.

I did another PD course through David Butler's NOI group that was more involved regarding the assessment and treatment of neural sensitivity. This course was "mobilisation of the nervous system". The main tests I would perform were the straight leg raise, which I would perform with the patient in side lying, the median nerve sensitivity test, and the slump test. Neural testing can be simple, but the hard part is knowing what you are feeling for.

When I am assessing neural sensitivity I will always test bilaterally, to gain an idea as to whether a neural test is symptomatic or asymptomatic. Positive signs include pain and a pulling sensation which the patient feels, which increase in intensity as you extend the knee or elbow with your test. You can couple this test with sensitising manoeuvres which include neck, hand, hip or foot movement depending on which test you are performing, or palpation of the lumbar spine erector spinae muscles or upper traps, again depending on which test you perform.

If I could recommend one skill apart from palpation that I feel is integral to be proficient with, it is definitely neural tissue testing and treatment. In routinely testing each patient's neural tension, irrespective of their presenting symptoms, I find patients with plenty of positive tests for neural tension. This allows me to treat these patients with the appropriate manual therapy, give them effective exercises to settle down their neural sensitivity, and educate my patient as to what is contributing to his pain presentation.

Neural pain tends to be severe, constant, worse with movement, easily stirred up, takes a while to settle down after the provocative activity, and tends to flare up with treatment. Consider the patient who has sciatica, or who has had a whiplash injury. Normally his pain is constant, and gets worse with insidious body movements which should not normally be painful. He has trouble sleeping comfortably and his pain is severe.

Neural pain does not need to be sharp, shooting pain either. Most people I treat who test positive for neural tension talk about an ache in a certain part of their body which can move around, and which they find hard to localise.

So start to test as many people's neural tension as possible, with the goal of differentiating between a normal test and a positive test, so when you come to treating a patient who you believe has neural sensitivity you don't miss it, otherwise your treatment results will not be as good as they should be![3]

REFERRED PAIN VERSUS COMPENSATION

This chapter is my opinion only (as is the rest of this book), and I would like to create a point of discussion around the topic of referred pain versus compensation.

At university we learned about referral patterns for tissue pathology, examples of which include intervertebral disc and facet joint referred pain. I was always interested by this particular phenomenon, but even more interested when, as a young physio, I applied this concept without great results for my clients in terms of pain relief or resolution of their condition.

As the years have passed and I have treated more patients, I believe more so in a model I call *compensation*, to explain why a person's pain and a person's problem are not in the same area.

Let's use the common example of people with lower back and buttock pain. Some believe that their pain into the buttock is a traditional somatic referred pain, others will say that the buttock pain is due to compensation, which to me means that the buttock pain is there due to a pre-existing problem before the back pain which has woken up, or the way the person is moving due to having back pain is excessively loading or changing the biomechanics through the buttock region.

Of course such a theory is very difficult to prove, and I concede to the advocates of clinical research that I may never prove that this phenomenon of compensation does actually exist, how to measure

---

3   For some further reading on neural pain and neurodynamic physiotherapy
     I recommend prominent physio David Butler and his progressive group of physios
     at the Neuro Orthopaedic Institute.

and quantify it, and how randomised double blind studies can either prove or disprove the existence of compensation.

But coming back to the person with back and buttock pain: I have observed countless times in my career that the primary problem will invariably settle down, and I need to then treat the secondary or compensatory problem as the person's injury settles, in order to help the person get back to being pain free and back to her goals. I've found that when I believed and followed the referred pain model and only treated the source of pain I was selling the patient short, and we were generally ceasing treatment before the patient became pain free. The person with back pain was walking away with no back pain but continuing low-level buttock pain when I followed the referred pain model.

My desire to assess my client's whole body and find these secondary areas of compensation and treat them as the patient is recovering from the primary injury is one of my clinical secrets in my pursuit to give my patient the best results possible.

I find people with neck pain have compensatory zones in their thoracic spine and shoulder, people with shoulder pain generally have thoracic and arm compensatory zones, thoracic spine tends to be shoulder compensation, lumbar spine can be SIJ, hip, hamstring or thoracic compensation, pelvis and SIJ issues can be influenced by any body area from the thoracic spine down (as a force transfer joint in your body), knees are generally influenced by hips and feet, and feet can be influenced by anything from the thoracic spine down also.

My message to you is to take secondary zones of compensation seriously, especially as your patient is recovering from her primary injury. Sometimes I find as physios we "have the blinkers on" and only focus on the main area of injury. Every time my patient returns for an appointment I assess the initial injury and the secondary compensation zones, and this gives me absolute clarity about what I need to achieve with my patient in this treatment session.

EVIDENCE-BASED PRACTICE DOES NOT EQUAL RESEARCH

I recall reading a publication released by the National Health and Medical Research Council (NHMRC), an arm of the Federal Government, entitled "Evidence-based management of acute musculo-skeletal pain".[4] Did you know that the two best evidence-based treatments for acute lower back pain that have been proven to work better than placebo treatment are advice to stay active, which is one of the hallmarks of modern physiotherapy practice, and (wait for it) "heat wrap therapy"? If all we espoused was evidence-based treatment of acute lower back pain we might as well pack up our treatment plinths and give all of our patients suffering from acute lower back pain a $15 heat pack and go home!

---

4   https://www.nhmrc.gov.au/_files_nhmrc/publications/attachments/cp95_evidence_
     based_management_acute_musculoskeletal_pain_clinicians_131223.pdf

I will give you some other examples from the same publication of level 1 (the highest level of evidence) evidence-based treatments for other areas of the body: pulsed electromagnetic therapy for acute neck pain, and ultrasound for calcific shoulder tendonitis. I don't know about you but I wouldn't use these treatment modalities in a consultation.

So is using these research-proven modalities best practice just because they have supporting level 1 evidence? In this chapter I would like to expand on what evidence-based practice actually is, as after doing some research and reading a particularly good article about evidence-based practice by Chris Worsfold, this helped to enlighten me.[5]

Chris discussed how he was so blinded by research and trying to fit his patients into certain profiles that allow a research-based approach to help them that he confused them, they never came back, and the intervention he was hoping to perform with them never happened.

I was a critic of evidence-based practice when I held the incorrect belief that evidence-based practice was the same as what I understood clinical research in the physio world to be. There will be physios among you who will have the same belief that I used to have: evidence-based practice equates to research – they are the same thing.

I would like to enlighten you, as I have previously been enlightened.

WHAT IS EVIDENCE-BASED PRACTICE?

Evidence-based practice is a combination of three different elements in the physio world. The first element is best research evidence, the

---

5   www.chrisworsfold.com/how-to-cure-evidence-biased-physiotherapy.

second element is clinical expertise, and the third element is patient values and preferences.

Now I'm aware I am leaving myself open to enormous criticism here from staunch supporters of clinical research, and I understand that if I don't advocate research above all else I may be no better than the homeopaths and other professions who have fallen victim to studies proving that what they do has no clinical benefit. But what about the benefits of clinical expertise and taking into account a patient's values and preferences? Do research findings translate to success in the consult room?

Clinical research is not the be all and end all. The number of clients I have treated and have had referred to me over the years by GPs and orthopods who have knee pain and have been prescribed nothing but VMO strengthening exercises, and their knee pain persists, astounds me. If we do only what research suggests we should do we are selling our patients short.

What I do with these people is assess all of the muscles above and below the knee, find out which muscles are tight and weak, release and strengthen these muscles, and progress their treatment, exercises, gym and function as we make improvements in their pain and physical state. This is an example of adding elements two and three (from above) of evidence-based practice: clinic judgment, and patient beliefs and preferences.

I believe that in the complicated scope of dealing with people presenting with all types of pain and injury there is no such thing as "by the book" intervention. My experience also tells me that patients don't know or care about research – they just want to get better.

USING YOUR CLINICAL JUDGMENT

As physios we are always trying to prove ourselves. Who are we proving ourselves to? The medical profession? Society? Ourselves?

Instead of proving ourselves to all and sundry, I would challenge you instead to improve your process-driven thinking with a couple of simple questions.

When a patient comes in presenting with pain, I like to consider the following:

- What **caused it**? Which movement faults, old injuries, biomechanical abnormalities, repetitive movements, areas of stiffness/weakness in the patient's body, negative beliefs, fears and thoughts?

- What does **the patient want from me**? This can generally be broken into four questions a patient has for most health practitioners: what is wrong? Can you help me? How long to recover? How can I help myself?

- What are the **main physical asterisk signs** I can find in their body? Both close to and away from the site of pain.

- What is my **priority with treatment**? Instant relief? A diagnosis? Self-management tools? Education? Or just me listening to their problem? If you are unsure about this, ask your patient – they will tell you what they want.

- Regardless of the result of my intervention at the first appointment, **what am I doing next to help my patients** if they get either great results, some results, or even get worse after my intervention?

This last point of early planning for each outcome between sessions is what I call clinical judgment.

A simple example of this approach is a patient with trochanteric bursitis presenting with severe lateral hip pain. I will generally have two or three sessions working on loosening and strengthening muscles in this region to reduce biomechanical faults that have caused this. Given this condition responds very well to steroid injections I will generally draw a flow chart very early on in the treatment process for the patient, explaining that if the treatment goes well we keep treating him, and if not we refer to his GP for an ultrasound scan and potentially a guided steroid injection if bursitis is in fact found on the scan.

This forward planning approach only comes with experience, and I have found that with good training, physios can be forecasting these types of conditions within six months of beginning in private practice.

From your patients' perspective this type of forecasting positions you as the expert in their eyes and they have instant confidence in you and will follow your recommendations, as opposed to the "by the book" approach I tried early in my career where I used only research-proven techniques and then had no idea how to respond if my patient wasn't getting better.

So after obtaining a proper understanding of what evidence-based practice actually is, I am completely supportive of this approach. Make sure you remember that evidence-based practice is not one and the same as best research evidence – never lose sight of your clinical judgment and each patient's beliefs and values.

CHAPTER 11

THE DIAGNOSIS: KEY TO THE CONSULT

Every day in my practice I am reminded of the power of a meaningful diagnosis for my patients. They come in to the clinic seeking relief, answers to their problems, insight and advice, and my professional opinion.

A GREAT PRACTITIONER IS A GOOD LISTENER

Young physios may not believe this, but I have performed many consultations where the patient doesn't even hop up out of the chair – we don't get beyond the subjective examination. This is not common and needs to be pre-addressed and framed properly with the patient, but for patients with a complicated condition who need me to understand where they are coming from and listen to their complicated history and story, my listening ear is the most valuable thing I can provide in the consultation. A great practitioner is a good listener.

I will give you an example of a good diagnosis. I recall treating a man of about 50. He came in to the clinic and gave me a referral from his GP that was about nine months old. His condition was annoying him greatly and he was unable to run for exercise, which he had previously enjoyed greatly, but he simply hadn't got around to making his appointment to see me. This was for a number of reasons, and I decided to ask why this was. He had seen several physios in the past. One of them had put this tingly machine on his leg, which did nothing. Another told him he had weak glutes, but he found the exercises complicated and he didn't know if he was doing them right, and they gave him no relief, so he gave up.

At the start of our consultation I asked him if it was okay if I did something different regarding his assessment, treatment and recommendations, and he was happy with that.

The man had constant pain in his left hamstrings as well as soreness in his outer left foot, which stopped him running. When I assessed him he walked fine and his glutes tested strong enough on both sides. All I found on his gait assessment was a left calf which was weaker than the right side. I then performed my tests for neural tissue sensitivity, and his left lower limb neural tissue was extremely sensitive. I then started asking him about any back pain, and he said he had this spot half way up his back on the left side which had been tight for 10 years, as he used to play golf five times a week and this had caused the pain. I also asked him about his lungs, which I do for any patient who has mid thoracic stiffness. He said he had a severe lung condition for two to three years which may have also contributed to his pain. Following this, I assessed his breathing pattern and found he was breathing too much from the shoulders and not enough from the lower ribcage.

The man found this assessment process fascinating and he asked lots of questions as we went, to which I gave him simple and easy-to-understand answers. I gave him a very simple breathing exercise which he understood, and asked him to do it several times a day. He was confident and had clarity with this exercise, and he knew he would not find it too challenging.

I informed him next that I wanted to see him for another appointment in a week to see how he was progressing. He now seemed excited about physiotherapy and what I could offer him, as I had gained his confidence by giving him a diagnosis that was meaningful.

When I asked, "Do you have a sore back here?", after I touched his mid thoracic spine, and he hadn't previously told me he had suffered stiffness in that area over the past 10 years, I instantly gained trust with my patient. He felt like I knew what I was doing, and therefore he had confidence in me. I understood his problem and how to help him get better. He was now on side with me, and this is the type of "wow" factor you can often give a patient in a consultation that will result in them telling all of their friends what happened in that consultation, and singing your praises to their friends and family.

After restoring a normal breathing pattern and strengthening his weak calf he was pain free and could now run again. I had restored his faith in physiotherapy, which for me is a very satisfying element of what I do when someone has previously achieved less than optimal results with physiotherapy, and has reverted to seeking help from other allied health professions that do not have the complete approach that physiotherapy has regarding assessment, diagnosis, treatment and self-care.

EVERYTHING I DO IN A CONSULTATION, FROM START TO FINISH

Let me explain to you everything I do in a consultation, from start to finish. One of my mentors, Paul Wright (owner of PhysioProfessor), has detailed a multi-step perfect consult for those who want a bit more detail on this concept. Here is my version.

When my receptionists book a patient in for a new consultation they always take the person's first name, surname, phone number, and note the part of the body the patient is having trouble with.

On my practice management software, new patients show up with a specific marker beside their name, so I know that they are a new patient. My receptionists detail the part of the body on the patient's electronic file, and I take note of the patient's first name and body part before I leave my consult room.

I leave my consult room and go out to the waiting room. I generally head to the receptionist first, who will have the paperwork from the new patient at the ready for me. I then call the patient's name (first name generally), and approach the patient.

I will always shake hands, and introduce myself by saying, "I'm Nick, nice to meet you". It's important to break the ice. You need to consider that the patient may be scared, distressed, nervous, or suffering from a state of real physical discomfort.

Next step is I lead the patient to my consultation room. Initially I take the lead, and then I allow the patient to walk in front of me once it's obvious where to go. This allows me to observe the patient's gait, which I am going to follow up with anyway. Once the patient has entered my consultation room I invite her to sit, or sometimes stand if she is in severe pain and appears as though she can't sit comfortably.

I start by letting her know we are going to begin with a conversation where I get to know her, and I'm going to ask her a few questions to find out about the problem she is suffering from and how I can best help her.

We then do the subjective assessment. I have checked the new patient form she filled out prior to the appointment, which has a couple of really important details. The two parts of this form that are most meaningful to me are the sections that ask:

1 What is your reason for seeking our services today?

2 What do you hope to achieve from physiotherapy?

The answer to question one is normally a variation on one obvious core theme: the patient wants to get out of pain. Some people say it this explicitly. Some people want pain relief, others want something more specific, like a diagnosis or finding out what's causing their problem. I estimate that 8 out of 10 patients at Scarborough Physio and Health state that getting out of pain is the main reason for coming to us.

Question two is mainly trying to find out what the patient's goals are. Responses to this are quite varied. For more complicated problems people want a diagnosis and plan for how to reduce their pain and improve their health, some people have specific goals and deadlines they need to achieve, some people want to get back to work, and for others it can be as simple as being able to sit or sleep without pain, or run or walk pain free.

It's important to pay attention to this second point, as this is what motivates your patient. Do not forget this. This goal can be referred to as their "significant emotional event" (another Paul Wright-ism), which is the thing that drives them most. If you miss this point you miss a major way of connecting with your patient.

Back to the subjective examination. I generally ask the patient several questions about her current symptoms and injury history. I don't want the patient to be too long winded and ramble on, so when I detect signs of rambling, I interrupt nicely and ask my next question, which generally brings her back to the point.

I next ask her about her life and daily routine, so I can understand how the things that she does every day might contribute to her current problem. Finally, I ask her questions about her general medical health, which assists me to complete the picture. While asking these questions I type at my computer, but I make sure to acknowledge the patient often with nods, eye contact, affirmative remarks, and plenty of good-quality active listening and communication. Patients expect you to face towards them, look at them, and listen to them.

I then explain that we are going to do some simple movement tests, and I will check the part of her body where the problem is, which is the physical assessment. So that my patient is comfortable during the physical assessment, I always explain what I would like her to do. I am always firm with my touch without pushing hard on the patient's body. I consider a reassuring and confident touch to be an essential part of physio assessment and treatment. If she does not understand what to do, I do the movement first, and then invite her to copy me by trying the movement herself.

When I conduct my palpation, I start with the patient standing so I can check lots of different body areas quickly, and then I move into a more specific palpation assessment where the patient is sitting, side lying, or supine or prone lying. I constantly ask the patient, "How does that feel?", and I am also looking for signs of discomfort on her face, or withdrawal or sensitivity when the patient moves her body or if I push on a certain area.

After I've performed the assessment, I normally have the patient sit on the side of the bed, and I let her know I have to note down the major findings of the assessment, generally four or five major positive signs, or asterisk signs. (An asterisk sign is a term I was taught by Michael Ridgway, which means a positive assessment finding – a finding generally regarding a patient's posture, movement, functional testing or palpation.) I explain to her what these main findings mean, and this gives her some idea of what is wrong with her.

Here's an example:

Jane, when you bent over yesterday you strained your lower back. I found that you have protective muscle spasm right at the base of your lower back. It causes you pain to sit and bend forward, and you are very tender when I touch the lowest joint on the right side of your lower back, which is where two vertebra meet. You haven't broken this area; it is a soft tissue injury – a strain. What we will try to achieve with treatment is to reduce the pain in this area and get you moving better so you can sit and bend without any pain. How does that sound?

You can then move on to treatment. In the initial consultation I like to keep the subjective, physical assessment and treatment separate, but as I get to know the patient I tend to be able to merge the physical assessment and treatment and still achieve great results.

When you treat the patient you need to be always mindful of her pain and comfort. If lying prone, her face needs to be comfortable on the physio bed, her shoulders generally need support with towels, and I always put a pillow under her shins also. When she is side lying, I put a pillow between her knees, and when supine I make sure that her head is slightly elevated on the pillow so she can see what I'm doing.

I will generally perform manual therapy initially, which may include spinal PPIVMs or PAIVMs, trigger point therapy, a Mulligan SNAG, a muscle release or muscle activation with movement, or a neural glide. I will then generally reassess some of the patient's asterisk signs, and see if she is moving any better. If the patient has a difficult condition, I warn her that she will not always move better after the treatment, although most patients do move or feel better with the right treatment method.

After manual therapy I will then generally prescribe simple exercise. It is generally only one or two exercises in the first consult, for a couple of reasons. I don't want to confuse the patient by giving her too many things to think about or do, and I also want to confirm my diagnosis with treatment and exercises that are very specific at the initial consultation. When I was a younger physio and I gave a sheet of exercises to the patient and asked her to do the exercises three times a day, I failed to consider how long these exercises took to do, how the patient could fit them into her schedule, and which exercises were most helpful for her condition. And be aware that if the exercises are confusing or painful then the patient won't do them.

Throughout the consult I provide the patient with plenty of helpful advice regarding the nature of the condition, things she should or shouldn't be doing, and I address any fears or negative beliefs she may have regarding her injury. The patient is generally very appreciative of simple advice, especially if you can explain to her why she shouldn't be doing certain things. I relate the importance of the treatment, exercises and advice back to her significant emotional event, to make sure she is on board with the treatment plan.

I then give my patient strong recommendations as to the things she needs to do to help her recover. I write these things down on a piece of A4 paper with my company letterhead on it, and give this to the patient. After answering any last questions from the consultation, I ask the patient to rebook using the strategy I detail in chapter 15, *When do I see you again?*

Finally, I thank the patient for her time, and ask her to see the receptionist to book the next appointment, and remind her that if she has any problems or questions after the consultation she is most welcome to contact our clinic. At the same time I Skype my receptionist and – after checking my electronic diary as to my availability – let the receptionist know I want to see the patient on day X and time X, which is a mutually agreeable time for the patient.

THE FOLLOW-UP CONSULTATION

I won't go into too much detail regarding the follow-up consultation, but again I welcome the patient by name, ask her how her day has been so far, and when she enters the consult room I ask her how she has been and what has happened since the initial consult. I'm quite efficient with my time for the subjective assessment in the follow-up consultation, and spend most of my time doing physical assessment and treatment, where I tend to blend assessment and treatment more.

I will again regularly refer to the patient's significant emotional event, and make sure she feels like she's on track to achieve her goals and treatment plan. If she doesn't feel she is on track I will try to determine what barriers are holding her back.

* * *

This consultation pattern may vary according to a patient's condition, her individual needs, or any barriers or objections which may present early on in the patient's care.

CHAPTER

12

BEING REALISTIC ABOUT YOUR LEVEL OF EXPERIENCE

TEN THOUSAND HOURS

As I've mentioned previously, it's often said that it takes ten thousand hours to gain proficiency in any particular field, especially in the professional world. I'm now going to expand on this topic to help put this in practical terms for young health practitioners.

With all of the hype around starting your career, there is definitely an element of having to keep your feet on the ground. At the end of your degree you feel superhuman and like you know everything. But, after you saw your first real patient in your first paid employment as a physio, I'm sure the feelings you had about where you were in your career brought you back down to earth. I definitely felt this way. If you don't feel this way you are either far advanced from where most people are when beginning their careers in a health industry or something is very wrong and you consider yourself to be a lot more proficient than you actually are – and this can be quite dangerous, as an important aspect of being a quality health practitioner is knowing your limitations in terms of your scope of practice.

Anyway, back to the ten thousand hours. Suppose you work a 40-hour week, and let's round a normal 48-week working year up to 50 to keep the numbers round; so, 40 times 50 equals two thousand hours. So, how many years doing two thousand hours a year of clinical work will it take to become proficient? This might seem obvious; the answer is five, isn't it? (All those years of study do pay off.)

But think about this. The answer is only five if you also spend serious amounts of time, effort and money on your continuing education. As well as growth by clinical experience you need to grow through mentoring, reading, online education, and my preferred method of hands-on courses. I try to attend at least three hands-on two- or three-day professional development courses every year.

If you do not continue to grow in your profession every year, you are simply repeating the first year of your training over and over again. It is often said that a person with twenty years' experience in their field either has 20 years' experience or has repeated the first year twenty times.

After five years of my physio career I felt I was starting to "get it", and it did take this long for me to feel comfortable and that I no longer felt signs of my inexperience all around me on a daily basis. At this stage I felt like my patients were listening to me, and more importantly, I was listening to them. They were getting consistent results, and I knew why and could predict positive results, and also see warning signs in a patient's presentation which might result in him getting a poor outcome.

Make sure you don't repeat the first year of your career twenty times over!

LOWER YOUR EXPECTATIONS

Don't expect to be the best straight away – you are not the best, and neither am I. It is dangerous to think you are.

It is said that there are two types of physios in private practice early in their career: those who know everything, and those who fear they know nothing. Guess which one is more of a potential danger to their clients – you guessed it, the first one!

I believe that these two different mentalities are effectively magnifications of your pre-existing mental state, of either natural overconfidence, or natural underconfidence. I was definitely leaning towards overconfidence. At the start of my career I thought I knew everything. Every patient failure I had (and there were many in my first couple of years) helped to erode this belief and give me the reality check I needed. The benefit of this was that I became vulnerable, recognised my weaknesses, and this gave me the thirst for learning that I still have.

A concern of mine is young physios who are underconfident without justification. Most physios I meet have a level of technical proficiency that allows them to treat 95% of the patients they will come across in their daily practice. But they lack the ability to effectively help the more difficult patients, and this significantly affects their confidence. What they don't realise is that these patients are difficult for all of us – experienced and inexperienced physios alike.

Young physios have no frame of reference, unless they have a reasonable amount of experience working in a private practice doing reception, massage or work experience. This leads many young physios to have the incorrect belief they must "fix" their patients in the first one or two sessions, otherwise they are a failure.

One of the first things I do with the young physios who work with me is let them know that it's unrealistic to have this belief that they must "fix" a patient in two sessions. A challenging observation I have made is that the more experienced the physio, the more consultations they will have with their patients. My belief around this is that more experienced physios help their patients get closer to their end results courtesy of optimal communication and relationship building, setting realistic expectations for the patient, and great treatment outcomes.

If you are a less experienced physio, first you need to acknowledge that you have no point of reference regarding the likely resolution of any condition. This is something that only experience or mentoring can provide, and there is no way that before you start physio work in private practice you can have any idea as to the likely resolution of a patient's presenting condition. I would even go so far as to propose that physios with different skillsets and different special areas of interest would have trouble crossing over into different clinic environments – for example, private practice versus hospital, community rehab versus paediatrics – even if quite experienced.

So young physios – don't worry. Your patients do not expect you to fix them in the first one or two sessions. As an experienced physio, if I find out that they expect this, I have the communication skills to either help address this limiting belief or refer them to a physio (generally my competitors) who can help them achieve the miracle cure that they desire.

Once you acknowledge this limiting belief in yourself it is like lifting a weight off your shoulders. As physios in private practice no-one puts more pressure on us to achieve great client outcomes than we do. Imagine if one of your beliefs is the biggest thing limiting your happiness in your daily practice?

At the end of the day I walk out of my office knowing I have done everything I can to help all of the people within my circle of control, and this is a truly liberating feeling.

PART

III

PEOPLE

IMPROVING YOUR COMMUNICATION SKILLS

What is the difference between a physio who gets great results for clients and a physio who has treated patients who stop coming to treatment and go away telling their friends "physio didn't work" or "that physio couldn't help me"?

You guessed it: good communication skills.

When we learn to optimally communicate with our patients we build trust, improve compliance and therefore outcomes, and nurture the kind of long-term relationships with our patients that are the cornerstone of private practice success.

Remember that your patients are people you will have multiple contacts with over the years for different problems and conditions, both with themselves, and their families and friends. If we do not communicate well, we run the risk of not helping our patients and them losing confidence in us, and potentially the physio profession as a whole.

So what is optimal communication and how do you communicate optimally?

Read on to find out what section three of the Physio Success Quadrant is all about.

THE ART OF THE PERFECT PITCH

Let me ask you this: how do you pitch yourself as a physio or a clinic owner? The situation I am talking about is your scripted response when someone you meet for the first time in a professional or social situation asks the well-worn question, "So, what do you do?"

Until recently, people would usually respond quite literally: "I'm a doctor", "I'm a plumber", and so on. Then some bright spark in the world of marketing started to encourage people to give an embellished but non-specific response. Some of the ones I've heard include, "I make dreams come true", "I change the world", "I help people find their inner peace", and some even more unusual responses. These are quite inspiring, albeit a little ambiguous.

Your initial response to this question needs to address the query in a practical way, but then you are allowed to let your creative side take over and tell the interested party how what you do is unique or special. If the person who asked the question looks at you strangely and doesn't ask a follow-up question, you know you have missed the mark.

How about this response?

Hi, my name is Nick. I own a physio and health clinic. I help people who have chronic and severe pain to find out why they are in pain, help them get out of pain, and get them back to living the lives they deserve.

If I get my pitch right, the next question should be, "And how do you do that?" That's the response I'm looking for. If you can get this response it allows you to elaborate and say something like:

Through gaining a deeper understanding of my patient's general health, medical history and daily routines, and by conducting a series of tests aimed at finding the person's problem rather than just their symptoms, I am able to gain remarkable results with treatment which can help my patient to achieve pain-free status with results that they never thought possible!

DO YOU KNOW YOUR WHY?

The next part of your pitch is the *why*. Do you know what your *why* is?[6]

Here's mine:

You would not believe the feeling I get when I first meet some-one with chronic or severe pain. Their life is in ruins. They are stressed, nervous, and fearful of the future. They are seeking answers. When a person starts to get rid of their pain, gets off the physio treatment bed and says, "Hey, that was easier than before", has a big smile on their face, and leaves their appointment feeling hope and empowerment, you would not believe the feeling that I get. I feel like I'm giving them their lives back. This is why I love treating people in pain. I love this more than treating famous sportspeople, celebrities, or people in positions of power or influence. Give me the patient who has had pain for 20 years, who has seen many different doctors without success, who has been told that this problem will be with them for life, and they just have to learn to live with it.

What is your *why*? Define it, start thinking about It, and see if it aligns with your chosen career as a physio. If your *why* involves status, wealth or fame, I won't go as far as saying you had better

---

6   If you're wanting to define your purpose and this is something that you feel is necessary to help with finding your calling, try reading the book *Start with Why* by Simon Sinek.

choose another career, but I will say that to achieve these things in physio you need to be thinking, learning, working and doing the hard yards early on. If you're still studying, you need to be a sponge and soak up all the wisdom and knowledge from your lecturers, you need to find yourself a mentor, and you need to be prepared to put in thousands of hours of tough slog with your purpose in mind.

As a physio, most importantly, you need to care about your patients. This must be part of your *why*. You may have heard this quote before:

> *People don't care how much you know until they know how much you care.*

If you only remember one quote from this book, remember this one.

LEARN A NEW LANGUAGE

Patients don't speak our medical language. Big technical words will confuse them. They are not impressed by medical speak, they are baffled by it. The knowledge gap between you and your patient is one of the most fundamental reasons a patient may not get the best results from physio care. It may be as simple as just not being able to understand what you are saying.

We all have that friend who is borderline autistic, and when you meet her at a party and ask her what she's been up to she gets so technical on you that your head spins, and you wish you hadn't asked. Well, spare a thought for your patients, as this is often how they feel throughout your consultation. They can walk out with their heads spinning, especially if they have come to see you in a partially compromised state due to being sleep deprived, stressed, or affected by analgesia for the presenting condition.

During my four years at uni I learned physio speak. I realised after two or three years on the job I was speaking a different language, and spent the next five years reprogramming. Effectively what I did was work out what was wrong with my patient, understand it myself in physio speak, then before I opened my mouth I translated it back into patient speak, before presenting my findings to my patient. Suddenly the patient understood what was wrong with him. This improved understanding helped him to trust me – I knew what I was talking about, and he believed it. His compliance improved – he would do the things I asked him to do. He saw results – and wanted more. Once I helped set him on the right path, he would send his friends and family – and anyone else who would listen – to see me.

The less experienced the physio, the more he will throw medical speak at his patients, and the less his patients understand, the less compliant they will be. Having spent years learning this language and implementing this language in your clinical practice, it's quite challenging to unlearn it, but the benefits are significant.

So how do you unlearn physio speak? Number one, catch yourself using it with your patients. When you catch yourself using it, in that moment observe your patient. Is she paying attention? Does she understand? Look at her eyes – are they following you? Ask if she understands what you just said. But, expect her to be a little defensive and not necessarily tell you the truth – she doesn't want to embarrass herself in front of you, or look stupid by not knowing what a partial supraspinatus tear is, let alone what a rotator cuff tear is, let alone what a rotator cuff is, when she came in fearing she had arthritis in her shoulder which was causing pain.

When you observe the patient response, elaborate and simplify:

You have a partial tear in your supraspinatus tendon. What this really means to you is the little thing that attaches the muscle to the bone is torn. Once the swelling settles down and we get all

> *of the muscles around this area working together, your pain will*
> *recede and you will be able to use your arm normally again.*

Again, watch the response, and ask if she understands.

Repeat this process until you believe you have drummed all of the medical speak out of yourself. The only challenge I have found is when you are then dealing with other physios and medical professionals who do speak medical speak as their main language, I may come across as being a bit simple, but I'm okay with this as I understand the purpose of communicating in this way.

THE BENEFITS OF ASKING GREAT QUESTIONS

My business coach regularly tells me that the quality of my life is determined by the quality of the questions I ask – both of others, and myself. I have definitely found this statement to be true. Instead of just giving my patients information, I ask them questions. This leads to the exact information they are searching for.

There is a saying that the person asking the questions has the power in a conversation. There is no better example of this than the job interview. It's a while since I've been on the receiving end of an interview, but I have conducted hundreds of interviews in the last five years.

Asking good questions is a sure fire way to be on the front foot with your patients, especially when they throw difficult questions at you. One of my favourite question sequences I go through with my patients goes like this:

Patient: "My doctor told me to stop coming to physio."
Me: "What do you want to do?"
Patient: "I'm not sure."
Me: "Do you think it's helping?"

Patient (most of the time): "Yes."

Me: "If it's helping, do you think there is any benefit in you stopping?"

Patient: "No."

The best part about this process is if you ask the correct series of questions, the person comes to the answer himself.

One of my favourite movies is *Inception*, starring Leonardo DiCaprio. If you haven't seen it, the theme revolves around Leo's character and his team going inside people's minds during their dreams, and planting an idea. The person then wakes up believing they have had the idea themselves, and the person acts on it.

This is a process of influencing a person.

It can be used both for good and evil, and I choose to use it for good.

To ask a good sequence of questions with your patient feels to the patient like you are giving him control, but if you are leading your questions in a certain direction you are actually still in control. The outcomes of this process include a stronger relationship, a higher level of trust, and more compliance from your patients.

Let's go through another scenario, this time with a patient who hasn't done the exercises (we've all had this one!). Let's compare two different approaches:

Scenario 1: Old-style communication

Physio: "Have you been doing your exercises?"

Patient: "Sorry, I forgot."

Physio: "You know you need to do them. Please make sure you do them this week – it is really important for your recovery."

Patient: "Okay."

Scenario 2: Asking great questions

Physio: "Have you been doing your exercises?"

Patient: "Sorry, I forgot."

Physio: "Did something happen in the last week that prevented you from doing your exercises as we discussed?"

Patient: "Well, actually they took a long time and I didn't really know what I was doing, and I felt like there were too many different exercises and I wasn't sure how each of them would help me."

Physio: "That's interesting. What would help you do better with the exercises this week?"

Patient: "If you showed me how to do them again and perhaps gave me just the two most important ones, I could commit to doing them like you said."

Physio: "This sounds good – let's do it."

Can you see how the second scenario led to increased trust and building the patient–therapist relationship, due to the fact the physio asked the patient why he was having trouble with the exercises, rather than just telling the patient what to do? Can you also see how a question sequence like this can improve compliance and the patient's results?

I make very few assumptions about anything these days. I just make sure I ask great questions when I'm trying to find out the info I need, and I am making sure I ask better follow-up questions as well, to really get to the root of the important info I am seeking from the conversation.

Try this with your patients; I'm sure you will find it helpful.

Exercise: Taking back the power

Great questions often start with the words "who", "what", "when", "why", "where" or "how".

One of my favourite sayings is:

"The person asking the questions has the power."

Next time you are involved in a difficult conversation with a patient or team member, when they ask you a question, try countering their question with another question – take the power back in the conversation.

When you ask the question, try using one of the six question starters above – I find "why" to be the easiest and most natural.

UNDERSTANDING YOUR PATIENTS

What does your patient believe is wrong with her? Why does she believe her pain is not going away? What does she believe caused her to be in pain in the first place? Did she just "sleep funny"?

Our patients sure can have some unusual beliefs about their pain and injury. Our beliefs are generally not the same as our patients', and more often than not are close to being the opposite. When two belief systems clash, many different outcomes can occur. The key word here is "clash".

Understanding is the missing piece of the puzzle to bridge the gap between your patients' beliefs and your beliefs. If you don't bridge this gap you run the risk of misunderstandings, objections, lack of trust, lack of compliance, and poor outcomes. Master this step and you can build the instant rapport we all crave with our patients.

ASKING THE BIG QUESTIONS

For me, this step is about asking the big questions. Here are some examples:

- How can I help you today?

- Why have you booked in to see me today?

- What do you expect from your consultation with me today?

- What are the main things you need to know today?

- Would you like me to explain what we are going to do today?

- What has/hasn't worked for you in the past?

- What are your main concerns regarding your pain/injury?

- Is there anything you are having trouble doing in your life due to this pain/injury?

- Is there anything coming up in your life that you need to be right for – any deadlines?

- Oh, so you have multiple injured areas. Today we only have time to focus on the main one that is troubling you, so where would you like me to start?

- What are the best days or times of day for you to come in for treatment?

- How did you find out about me and our clinic?

Building a bridge of understanding starts with removing doubt. These questions remove doubt. When you remove doubt it also helps you gain laser focus as to what you need to achieve in the consultation, especially if it's the initial consultation – you only get one chance to make a great first impression.

One of my favourite sayings is, "seek first to understand, rather than to be understood," from Dr Steven Covey. By seeking first to understand we fulfil the caring aspect of being a physio.

Any physio with a busy caseload can naturally find it hard to deliver the best results with every single consultation, especially if you are seeing lots of new clients whose problems you are not yet familiar with, and also if you are early in your career and not yet familiar with the significant variety of conditions you will see in your daily practice. The other benefit of asking these types of questions is it takes the guesswork out of the situation and provides certainty for both you and the patient.

I personally enjoy knowing that giving my patients the maximum degree of certainty within their consultation minimises the opportunity for uncertainty between the consultations. You might be surprised when people are in pain how vulnerable they can be to suggestion, especially from friends, and I have seen many patients over the years who as well as physio will have chiropractic or some other type of alternative medicine at the same time as seeing me for an injury. This is not a bad thing, but it is extra important in these circumstances for the patient to value the relationship with you and your ability to help him with the main problem for which he is seeking your services.

When you understand your patients they will become raving fans, and every physio and clinic can do with more raving fans; they fill your books up with their family and friends. More about raving fans later.

PROVIDING STRONG RECOMMENDATIONS

In private practice it is important to provide patients with recommendations specific to the problem they are seeing you for. In a way it's similar to giving the patient orders. As their therapist, you are giving recommendations from a position of strength and knowledge, and it is this that your patient expects from you.

How do you give strong recommendations to a patient who is most likely older than you and with more life experience, especially when you are not 100% sure about what recommendations to give?

When considering what recommendations to give to your patient, you need to think with a value-adding mentality. You should always be thinking, "What can I do to add value to the consultation with my patient?"

It's easy for me as an experienced therapist to advise you to give your patient strong recommendations, as I have done this so many times before. Let me tell you about the value you provide in a consultation as a young therapist. Young therapists are enthusiastic, and have a strong desire to help their patients. You are generally more willing to listen to patients, and this provides more value to them than you can possibly know. Most patients have had experiences seeing doctors or specialists who virtually dismiss their concerns and just tell them what is wrong. Sometimes the patient is berated by the senior doctor, and told that the problem is all in her head, and that there is nothing that can be done about it.

As a young therapist you are giving patients something that doctors and specialists cannot give them: the time to form a relationship with you, and for them to be heard. Never underestimate the value of helping people to express their concerns about the particular problem for which they are seeking your help.

LISTENING TO YOUR PATIENTS

We all know how frustrating it can be when people don't listen to us, but this can be magnified when we are in pain or are uncertain about a health complaint. If you do this first step well and genuinely show you are listening to and understanding your patients, they will believe you understand their problem. They are then waiting for you to give a strong recommendation for the best way to fix their particular problem.

You can recommend many courses of action: rest, activity, treatment, exercise in many forms, activity modification, ergonomic advice, pain education, referral to a GP or specialist, imaging or medical equipment such as orthotics. You are only limited by your knowledge of the condition and of what would be best for the patient.

My advice for a young therapist is to recommend what you are familiar with. If you have a patient come in with acute back pain, you know that most of the time this problem will correct itself, with or without your expert care. We know that with acute back pain the person needs to take it easy for a few days, then gradually start to get active again, taking care with movements that exacerbate the pain. The patient generally benefits from painkillers initially, gentle stretching, avoiding sitting for too long, some simple core exercises, and education as to the nature of the condition and the fact that she will be able to overcome this problem and will not be in pain forever.

Advice is very powerful – do not feel that you need to do heaps of manual treatment in a consultation at the expense of providing an expert opinion. Some of the most insightful consultations I have had with my patients have been purely diagnostic and advisory in nature.

Give the advice that you feel comfortable and confident with, but make sure you deliver the advice with confidence. Confidence does not mean that you have to know how the patient will respond to your treatment: with the bulk of patients I see, I let them know what they should expect to feel after treatment, but I always say that this is not exactly what they will feel and not to worry if they are sore or something else happens.

Another of my favourite sayings is: "It is better to underpromise and overdeliver". In essence, this means don't promise your patient the earth and deliver less than you have promised. At the start of my career I was too overconfident with my recommendations as to how quickly my interventions would get my patients out of pain. Patients would come back disappointed, or worse still, would doubt my future recommendations. You are better to be a little conservative, especially at the first consultation, and be pleasantly surprised at the results.

So start practising your recommendations. Be confident, conservative, give lots of simple advice, and just because you think the advice may be too simplistic it does not mean that your patient knows what you know about the body!

DEMONSTRATING EMPATHY

I've had countless patients complain to me about an experience they had with a very senior medical specialist where they were treated rudely, rushed out the door in less than 10 minutes, and had to pay a bill upwards of $200! Specialists are very good at what they do, but they often lack empathy for their patients. The more of a specialist you become, I find the less of an ability you have to interact with the common person. I can see how this is possible – they are often performing lifesaving procedures and making life-changing diagnoses for their patients, and so something that a specialist perceives as a minor complaint may be felt by the patient as quite a major complaint. They are focused on problem solving, not relationships and connections. So, it's very important to put yourself in your patients' shoes and show some empathy for the concerns they have about their condition.

You can do a good job to demonstrate empathy through three very simple tricks in your consultation:

- mirroring

- reflective listening

- eye contact.

Mirroring is simply acting in a manner similar to your patient, to build trust. If they are loud and boisterous, I have found I can act like this to build trust quicker. If they are quiet and reflective, I lower my tone, slow down my speech and am more circumspect in my communication. Sometimes with this communication trick you even find yourself using similar language to your patient.

Reflective listening is my most powerful communication trick. When a patient says something to you, you say, "So what you're saying is …", and they reply, "yes". To make this work properly you need to listen closely, and make sure you really understand what they are saying before stating their own words back to them – this can backfire spectacularly if you are not well trained in this method.

The final empathy-building strategy of eye contact may seem overly simple, and I can further clarify by suggesting that you meet their eye contact. How often have you been to a GP and spoken to them while they type away at their computer, not looking at you the whole time? This is most important during your subjective examination, and even more important during your first meeting with the patient.

Now I am not suggesting you simply use tricks to falsely build empathy, but I will assume that you are doing this for the right reasons – to enhance your relationship-building skills with people you genuinely want to build strong bonds with.

DEALING WITH YOUR PATIENTS' PROBLEMS AND PAIN

DO YOU REALLY KNOW HOW THEY FEEL?

Do you like pain?

I don't.

We think we understand pain, having dealt with lots of people in pain, but I can honestly say, and I'm sure some of you who have suffered major injuries can tell me, that we really can't appreciate what our patients are going through unless we have experienced their symptoms for ourselves. This is never more true than when treating people with chronic or severe pain, who are losing sleep, feeling stressed or depressed, and are unable to do the things they need to do every day.

Like most people, I often used the throwaway line, "I know how you feel", and my patients were at least partially believing of this statement, given I'm a physio and know lots of people in pain.

But given that everyone's pain is different and affects people in such different ways, I decided to take the plunge one day and say to a chronic pain sufferer, "I may be a physio who helps lots of people with severe pain, but personally I can't begin to imagine how you feel".

The positive response was astounding from the patient; someone had finally acknowledged that no-one can possibly understand what they are going through, without walking a mile in their shoes.

Give this line a go and see how it works for you.

DON'T HURT YOUR PATIENTS

That's great advice, right? Now, practically in a consultation I attempt to cause minimal pain to patients in the assessment and in the treatment. I will also not give an exercise that exacerbates their pain – this will reduce their compliance. (There are some general contradictions to this, such as guides for low-level pain with certain eccentric strengthening exercises for stable tendonoses.)

Some patients who come into my clinic and who can hardly walk I tend to be very careful with, and my physical assessment with them tends to be very limited. If a patient is in severe pain and during your assessment you significantly irritate the pain, this puts you behind the 8 ball with your treatment. A simple, practical piece of advice for young physios is to be careful positioning these types of patients. Us more experienced physios generally have an example of when we were a young physio and we had a patient with severe back pain in a prone position, performed a treatment, and at the end the patient couldn't get off the bed. Personally I have never had to call an ambulance for these patients; I have several colleagues who have also had this happen to them, some of whom have had to call ambulances for these rather unhappy patients. Good luck asking the patient to pay their bill and rebook with you when they are wheeled out of your clinic on a stretcher.

Anyone with very severe low back pain I tend to treat in a side lying rather than a prone position, and very elderly people who have severe pain and very poor ability to transfer in bed I will even treat in a seated position. When I treat people with severe mobility impairments I will always favour positions that are easy for them and for me, rather than trying to get them into awkward positions where I can do a little bit more in terms of their treatment. I've found when I have made mistakes with these types of patients in the past it can cost me valuable time in the consultation, and this is time I can't get back.

Many of my patients say "no pain, no gain". While I say that I don't cause any of my patients pain, I'm happy to cause some low-level discomfort treating stable and non-irritable conditions; it is mainly the conditions where I don't know how they could respond that I am most careful with. I would recommend that for any condition you're treating where you don't have a reasonable idea how your patient will pull up, it's beneficial using the "less is more" approach, otherwise your receptionist may receive a call from the patient the next day complaining that you hurt him and you didn't let him know that he may pull up sore after the consultation.

HANDLING PATIENTS' OBJECTIONS

A vital skill to have in private practice, and also in life, is the ability to handle the complaints and objections that come your way. This has never been more evident than when you operate a business where you are dealing with the public. Patients have approached me with myriad objections in the past. Some of these objections relate more to their situation, and some of them may relate to experiences they had at our clinic.

Objections can be very simple, such as difficulty getting in for an appointment, car parking around the clinic, how long they had to wait to see their therapist, or other operational issues that do not relate to the time you are directly spending with the patient. Be aware that if you are the business owner you are directly responsible for all of these issues, even if you consider that you shouldn't have to be. For instance, most people's greatest objection with any medical practitioner is the punctuality of the practitioner. People hate being kept waiting, so be very mindful of being on time for your visits, or you will have plenty of objections.

Scarborough Physio and Health has a unique way of dealing with this particular objection. We offer an on-time guarantee – if we are late, the patient gets the appointment free of charge. It keeps me and our other therapists very accountable for our time.

You will also come across more major objections. Generally as a junior therapist these can include pain after treatment, a perceived lack of progress by the patient regarding his condition, a desire from the patient to see a more experienced therapist if one is available, and quite a few others.

Being a solo practitioner for the first five years of my career shielded me from the dent to my pride that was having my lack of experience brought into question. This does happen in clinics where there are multiple therapists operating, all of different skill and experience levels.

CHALLENGING CONVENTIONAL THINKING

The purpose of my book is to kickstart your brain and encourage you to challenge conventional thinking. I heard a great story about the incredible lady who started physio, Sister Elizabeth Kenny. She treated polio patients, and came across a patient who she didn't know had polio. She wired the doctor in the closest town, who instructed her to "treat as symptoms present". Instead of immobilising the person, which was the standard treatment for polio at the time, she treated this person with heat packs and exercise, and the rest is history!

Sister Kenny thought laterally, treated the patient as the symptoms presented, and used her best judgment. She was single-handedly responsible for pioneering our profession. If she was alive today I'm sure she would encourage us to treat each person as symptoms present, rather than to just ask the person where the pain is, and then keep our assessment to that region.

My many experiences in private practice have taught me that a patient's pain and his problem are often in distinctly different regions of the body. This was a very big learning curve for me. I will give you an example. A US musculoskeletal therapist I follow on Facebook wrote an interesting meme about the knee: "If your patient has patellofemoral pain and you treat the patella, you are an idiot!" I had a bit of a laugh at this; I believe what he was trying to say was instead of treating the patella you should assess the patient and analyse the movement dysfunction which caused the patella to be sore, instead of trying to do some magic treatment to the patella to make the pain go away.

CHAPTER
15

WHEN DO I SEE YOU AGAIN?

"When do I see you again?"

This is one of my favourite questions. When a patient asks you this, what are you going to say? What thought process is going through your head? Does this question scare you? What clinical justification do you use to respond to this question?

For a young therapist or new graduate, this is a very challenging question. After all, to be put on the spot like this and to have to give an immediate response can be somewhat overwhelming. I will take you through a rationale to help formulate a good response to this question.

THE VARIABLES IN REBOOKING A PATIENT

Let's brainstorm for a minute about this question. To start with, it's a great question, because the patient has already acknowledged that she needs to see you again – the question is, when? You have already achieved the first step as you have helped your patient and provided some value in your consultation. She's happy, and is now after further guidance and wants a follow-up appointment.

VARIABLE ONE: SEVERITY OF THE CONDITION

To answer this question accurately, you need to be on top of several variables. Variable number one is the severity of the person's condition. I believe this consideration should form the basis of the response. If the patient is in very severe pain and needs your help urgently, you should see her for another consultation again as soon as humanly possible.

Think of a professional rugby league player. When he injures himself, how many physio sessions does he do each day to recover as quickly as possible for the next game? Many elite athletes who are injured have three intense physio consults a day to achieve the best results.

But our patients are not all professional athletes. A follow-up appointment as soon as practically possible is generally made for the following day. This makes sense.

VARIABLE TWO: THE PATIENT'S AVAILABILITY

But what if variable two, the patient's availability, gets in the way? Patients have to work, they have family commitments, or they simply don't have time in their busy schedule. How do you compromise on best quality care? I must say this can be a challenging part of the job.

Based on the severity of the patient's injury you need to reach a mutually beneficial arrangement as to the date of his next appointment. Often if the injury is severe the patient will make time. If you want him to come back the next day or in two days' time, and you stress the urgency of this recommendation and how it will help him get rid of the pain in the least possible time, he will generally make time. He will duck out of work, or start later or finish earlier to fit your appointment in. He will shuffle, rearrange, find a family member to look after the kids, or cancel the lunch or day out. After all, getting out of pain is an extremely strong impulse. It's said that to relieve pain is a far greater human urge than to create pleasure. For example, if you had a headache, would you be more keen to have that headache go away, or would you rather go out to lunch with your best friend? Just make it stop!

VARIABLE THREE: YOUR AVAILABILITY

So, let's say you have achieved your goal and overcome variable two, and agreed that the patient needs to see you tomorrow and he will book an appointment. But it's a Friday at midday, and your clinic doesn't open on Saturdays.

What do you do now? Welcome to variable three – *your* availability. Before giving any recommendation, I will *always* make sure that my recommendation matches my availability. Situations that challenge my availability include days when I have no free appointments, weekends, conferences, and holidays, in that order. One consequence of helping lots of people in your community to relieve their pain is that you tend to become quite busy. The more people you see for appointments, the less availability you seem to have into the immediate future for more appointments. When I'm rebooking a patient I always check my diary for the day I would like him to return before I give the recommendation, to make sure I have options if that day is heavily booked. I want to give my patient the best recommendation possible for his problem, but it needs to fit in with my schedule.

If the best recommendation does not fit with my schedule, I want to make sure I have options. I can ask him to have a session with my very capable colleague (again based on checking availability) or one of our other therapists (including a massage therapist, counsellor or acupuncturist), he can commence pilates if he has a complaint that would respond well to core stability exercise, or I can give him some advice for self-management and activity in between my consultations with him.

MY GUIDELINES FOR REBOOKING

As you can see, I'm flush with options for how to help my patients best manage their problems. But I first need to be very clear in my own head regarding these options, my order of preference, my availability, their availability, and most importantly, what their injury generally calls for.

Some guidelines I use are:

- For a patient in **severe pain or with a severe problem**, such as nerve pain or a complicated injury, I will ask her to come back within two days.

- For a patient with **less severe pain**, or alternatively a patient with **severe pain and limited availability**, I will want to see him within three to four days.

- A patient who has **less severe pain or a less severe complaint** – for example, mechanical knee pain for which she needs strengthening exercises – I will generally see a week after her initial consultation.

- There are some patients I will see two, three or even four weeks after the initial consultation. These patients are rare, and are generally **not in much pain at all**, and are coming for a strengthening or balance programme. I generally recommend to these patients that they return in a timeframe that gives enough time for the exercises to have had some benefit – at least two weeks – so I can give them a higher level progression of their exercises.

A pattern that will often occur in a health-based business is that a patient will initially attend the clinic with severe pain. He may require three to five appointments in quick succession, often over a 7- to 10-day period. Once his pain becomes less acute and he requires less hands-on intervention, I then see him either twice or once weekly. As his treatment progresses over a four-week period after the initial pain has subsided, I start to space out his follow-up appointments with the philosophy of, *how long before the patient's pain comes back?*

I will give you a hypothetical situation. A patient with a bad back is getting better, and he finds that his back pain only gets worse towards the end of the week at work. I see him in a week and he is going well. I then make his next appointment for two weeks. If he goes well I space it out further to three or four weeks; if he doesn't go well I keep the appointment at two weeks; and if he flares up badly I see him again within a week.

Patients love this system as the recommendation is specific to them. Physios find this system helpful as it gives good clinical justification. Everyone wins. And we know when everyone wins, we get great outcomes and our job satisfaction increases.

TO REBOOK OR NOT TO REBOOK?

I remember attending a great one-day conference based on improving communication skills for physios. We had a really great presenter who was a lady who has owned private physio practices for over 20 years – she knew her stuff about the issues facing private practitioners. At the beginning of the day she started her presentation with what is often the elephant in the room: the fear of young professionals that they are "overservicing" their patients, which is effectively seeing them too often or for too many treatments.

A very interesting point she raised was: have a guess who sees their patients for more visits – the experienced practitioner or the new graduate practitioner? You guessed it – the experienced practitioner wins by a country mile!

This really blows the belief systems of young health professionals out of the water. Surely you would think that if experienced practitioners are seeing patients more often they are doing something unethical, overservicing them and are just after their money, or are simply not getting good results. How is it possible that a more experienced practitioner would need to see a patient for more visits to fix her? Doesn't this go against everything we are taught at uni? Fix them quickly, then get them off the books – they will get better so quickly they won't know what hit them.

Why do we need to equate helping people with their health, changing their lives and giving them a great value service with taking money out of their back pocket? Do we value ourselves and our service so little that we would prefer disgruntled patients to leave our clinic when we discharge them from our care while they are still in pain, to go onto Google and choose from a multitude of practitioners in their local area without the knowledge, expertise and care that we can provide to them?

So why do experienced practitioners see patients for more consultations than junior practitioner?

I believe there are two reasons behind this.

The first reason is the senior physio is clinically superior, and rather than just following a set protocol for treatment, for the more difficult patient whose recovery does not follow the typical recovery pattern and requires adaptability or a change of treatment pathway, the senior therapist is able to achieve this. Sometimes the most important part of treating a patient is when I feel I have "maxed out" the patient's recovery with one type of intervention or focus on one body segment, and I am able to reassess, explain to the patient why I am changing direction, and focus on a different segment of the body which is often removed from where the pain is. An example of this is as a person's shoulder pain improves, treating areas of the arm, cervical or thoracic spine when the shoulder signs improve and the pain is getting better, but still persists.

An extension of the above clinical skills is that when a patient trusts you he will come back until he feels he can self-manage his condition due to the great results he is achieving, but often he will also mention other problems that he didn't originally mention to you. Due to the results achieved so far, he will ask you to move on and help him with another problem.

The end result of this clinical success is the patient will then book his partner, parent or friend in with you. This is when you know you have done a great job.

The second reason a senior physio will have more consultations is their advanced communication skills. Many senior physios I know are not afraid to have the tough conversations with their patients, are happy to admit when they need to take a different approach, are better at getting to the bottom of what is really frustrating patients, and also better at understanding and inspiring their patients towards their goals.

Advanced communication takes mentoring, time and many mistakes to develop. Many of my favourite patients have started as people whose treatment direction was not clear or easy to start with, but we worked through their challenging problem together and came out the other side, forming a great professional friendship in the process.

So if you are a younger physio or a clinic owner who mentors young physios, please be aware that the fear of overservicing is a natural fear, and comes from the fact the young physio's identity has not yet shifted from student to clinician. This identity shift can take years, but through high-quality mentoring and experiential learning we can facilitate this positive shift.

If you are a junior practitioner and you want to practise your rebooking, please go to www.ultimatephysio.com.au and download a copy of our consultation plan template to use in your practice.

A PLAN FOR REBOOKING SUCCESS

The end of the initial consultation is, in my opinion, the most pivotal part of your patient–therapist journey. This is where you as the physio have the opportunity to give a recommendation. The physios who work at my clinic follow a template when they get to the end of the initial consultations, which helps greatly with rebooking.

My physios have a form with four headings on it:

- **Name:** to make patients take ownership over their plan.

- **Diagnosis:** in plain English, for them to understand and have a meaningful diagnosis, with limited medical jargon.

- **Recommendations:** what you want them to do – exercises, activity modification, lifestyle modification, other tests needed, and so on.

- **Plan:** your plan for their treatment, including approximate timeframe for their condition and any other services you will bring in; for example, massage, pilates, acupuncture, orthotics, gym or exercise physiology.

Our patients love their plans. Plans make it easy for them, and take away doubt. Another Paul Wright saying is "a confused mind always says no". The patient is coming to you for your advice and expertise; why should you go to jelly at the end of the consultation due to your negative beliefs?

Don't sell your patients short; give them a recommendation to help them gain optimal results from their treatment. Giving patients something to take with them after the consultation – even as simple as a piece of paper – gives them a point of reference between consultations with you. I give my patients more pieces of paper as I progress their treatment and exercises, and as I remove and consolidate their exercises to make sure they are doing the most appropriate exercises at every stage of their recovery, as a flaw I often see is that as patients get closer to 100% we don't update or modify their exercises to help them reach that magic goal they are seeking.

GIVING RECOMMENDATIONS LIKE AN OLD HAND

So what is the main difference between a junior and an experienced physio? A junior physio treats the patient's body, while an experienced physio treats the patient's mind. What do I mean by this? Read on.

I will give you the reality of the situation and the thought processes which I operated with as a young practitioner, and what I think now that I'm more experienced.

When I was a young physio operating in my own business I had unrealistic expectations about how quickly my patients should be getting better. After all, we had never been taught this stuff at university – we knew how quickly soft tissue injuries healed, but people are not just soft tissue!

I would project these unrealistic expectations onto my patients. I would treat someone coming in to see me who was suffering with severe pain (who would realistically take a couple of months to get back to normal) and I would feel that it was my responsibility to fix her in just one or two visits. When I did not achieve this I would become frustrated – why are you not getting better quickly! This would in turn frustrate the patient.

During consultations I would sometimes be too brief with my assessments and explanations. Because of this I did not understand the person's unique situation well enough – what she understood about her injury, how it was impacting on her day-to-day life, what her fears and frustrations were, and what she really wanted from me and her goals and hopes for the future. I treated patients far too quickly, and spent too much of the consultation doing treatment, which I thought was the magic bullet they needed; after all, this was the stuff we focused on at uni … it must be the stuff that works. It was all I knew how to do. I knew how to treat the body but not the mind.

If the patient was not 90% better in three or four visits, her expectations had been built up far too high by me and I had incorrectly made her think that she should be better by now. This dissatisfaction led her to giving up on treatment, seeking help elsewhere, losing hope altogether, or returning to her GP for more suggestions.

The pressure I was putting on myself to "fix" my patients was too great, and unnecessary. And on reflection, I realise that this pressure was not something that my patients were putting on me, it was completely self-inflicted. I was doing everything in my power to help my patients recover quickly.

What I really needed was to take a step back, understand their conditions better, be optimistic yet realistic, and give firm but flexible recommendations that empowered the patient but did not place unrealistic expectations on either the patient or me.

The way I treat my patients these days is far different. I treat the mind first and the body second – and patients really respond well to this approach. I spend longer at the start of our initial consultation understanding the person's problem and how it is affecting him, learning about his goals, problems and frustrations, and finding out what he is expecting from me.

Understanding what the patient wants from me helps me to determine how I treat him. Some people want to know what is wrong in their body, some just want a diagnosis, others don't care as long as you help them feel better. Some people just want exercises to do to help themselves, others want you to get rid of that tight muscle on the inside of their shoulder blade that keeps them awake at night.

Another good way to find out this information is to ask these questions on your initial assessment paperwork. At our clinic we ask questions about the patient's goals, what he wants to achieve in his treatment, and any other points which he considers to be important. My assessment and treatment are heavily geared towards addressing the patient's perceived main problems. I find that I probably perform half the treatment I used to do, but with better outcomes as it is more targeted towards the patient's goals and needs.

I used to assess the patient at the start of the consultation, perform three or four different treatment techniques, and not bother reassessing him for fear of not producing a meaningful change. These days I will do one treatment technique at a time and reassess the patient's main positive signs from the assessment as I go, so I can see which treatment techniques are producing the greatest changes – these techniques are working. I can then explain to the patient why these techniques work, and give him simple exercises geared towards achieving the same results for the patient as the treatment technique has achieved.

I used to give the patient a whole sheet of 10 exercises to do, and ask him to do the exercises three times a day. I didn't acknowledge that the exercises would take half an hour to do every time.

Have you ever known anyone to spend one-and-a-half hours a day doing physio exercises, especially when he doesn't necessarily feel the benefit of the exercises at the time? No chance. Then the patient returns, the young physio asks, "Have you done your exercises?", the patient guiltily responds "no", feels bad, and feels that this is the reason he is not getting better. Not a good start to the consult, and not the best way to build a healthy professional relationship with your patient, is it?

This is how I prescribe exercises these days. Give the patient one exercise, show him how to do it, get him to do it, write it down, take a photo or video of it for him, tell him why he needs to do it, and make sure it is addressing the main problem you are treating him for and that he knows this. Oh, and tell him you want him to do it X times a day for the first few weeks until he starts to improve, and after that he can start doing it less often. The number of patients who do your exercises will go through the roof, and their treatment results will improve dramatically!

You too can prescribe exercises like an old hand – just put yourself in your busy patient's shoes.

BUILDING STRONG PATIENT RELATIONSHIPS

BREAKING THE ICE

I went on a great conference a while back where the bulk of the people did not know each other. The lead speaker at the conference knew that we would all be more productive and would enjoy the conference more if we all got to know each other.

Instead of asking us to turn to the person on our left and right and say hello, like you do in church, he asked us to do a great exercise which was similar in principle to speed dating. Half of the room stayed seated and had a spare chair next to them, and the other half of the room rotated around the chairs. You would spend two minutes with each person, where you would choose to ask one of five questions on a small piece of cardboard. You could ask them questions about their goals, dreams, daily life, work, and the like. The questions were meaningful and really helped to break the ice.

It was great to get to know these physios in a more personal way. Too often our standard questions are framed around concepts like, "What do you do?", or, "Where do you live?" These are not open-ended questions, and so responses to these questions tend to be short and sharp, and not conversational.

I pride myself on my ability to ask open-ended questions when meeting people and wanting to build a relationship and find out more about them. I also pride myself on being able to politely interject when a patient is rambling on, and asking a closed-ended question to which he can only answer yes or no. I think all health professionals need this skill, if only to improve our time management.

GOOD RELATIONSHIPS ARE ALL ABOUT TRUST

In this modern world of instant friendship at the drop of a hat, relationships can often be seen as a disposable commodity. After all, how many Facebook friends do you have? How often do you actually get to see these people, really get to know them, and find out what means the most to them and what is going on in their lives? You might call me old fashioned but I honestly do not see "friendship" in our society today in the same light as I did when I was growing up. Your friends were people you saw at least every week, you did stuff together, got into trouble doing stupid things, had fun, mucked around, and really got to know the ins and outs of each other's personalities.

I would rather have a few close friends than a list of 1,000 friends, none of whom I ever see. Real friendship is genuinely knowing and caring about someone's life.

In my experience, this is what our patients want from us. The thrill they get when you remember their kids' names, or their favourite hobby or sporting team, or ask about other things that are significant to them – that is a real relationship.

I'm not in any way suggesting you breach your professional duties as a physio and go out to the pub with your patients, but remember your patients don't care how much you know until they know how much you care. This principle is the cornerstone of my practice, and until you live by this principle you will never have a waiting list as long as your arm of clients wanting to see you.

Trust is a commodity that takes years to earn, but only seconds to destroy. Think about the people you trust in your life – your family, partner and close friends. The circle of trust often does not extend very far outside that group. What about your Facebook friends? Would you trust them with your most guarded secrets?

You need to be a person your patients trust. You need to be a pillar of integrity with their personal and medical information, and you need to make them feel they can trust you implicitly. I value my professional relationship with my patients greatly, and I believe that you can create relationships with your clients where you treat them as valued friends but maintain a professional distance that allows for positive interactions.

Remember, you are their confidante, adviser, and sometimes a shoulder to cry on. The more seriously you take this concept into your clinical practice, the more you will be known in your community as the person to see. Word-of-mouth referrals will flow from your existing client base, and the good words your patients share about you will help in creating new relationships with first-time clients.

THE CUSTOMER IS ALWAYS RIGHT. RIGHT?

When you were young did you ever have a job in either the retail or hospitality sector? Most people I know have worked in these sectors early in their working lives, to get some experience in the workforce or just to earn some loose change to fund their next social outing.

If you have worked in either of these sectors, or even if you haven't, no doubt you have heard the saying, "The customer is always right". I will add a caveat to this statement: "The customer is always right, *when it's in their best interests to be right*".

What I mean by this is the following. As an inexperienced practitioner we tend to bend to our patients' wills. We at times offer to give them what they want. I remember countless consultations with strong-willed patients at the start of my career. Some of them had quite scary and overbearing personalities. They would come into my office and say, "My back is out – I think I need a massage", or, "I need some ultrasound", or, "I really think hamstring stretches would fix my problem".

Not always having the confidence to properly diagnose my patient, I would sometimes succumb to their perceived needs. But afterwards, I felt a bit empty. Aren't I the therapist? Isn't the patient supposed to be listening to me, following my instructions, and getting great results?

How long did it take until I stopped bending to my patients' wills? I will tell you simply: I stopped bending to their wills when the instructions they gave me did not produce the results they deserved!

THE TRUTH THEY NEED TO HEAR

I honestly feel it took me about five years to become a confident private practitioner. Without confidence, you cannot tell your patients the honest truth they need to hear. Now I will clarify by saying that the honest truth is always delivered with empathy, tact and my patient's best interests at heart. You see, being a private practitioner is somewhat like being your patient's psychologist at the same time. You patients will need education, advice, a sympathetic ear, they will break down on you occasionally, and tell you things you didn't really need to know.

A part of the job I really love is when a person seeks my services, and comes in and has all of these confused preconceived ideas about what she needs. She has heard what has worked for her friend, read about someone on the internet who had a similar condition, or she saw an article or a story on TV about this great new therapy to cure her pain.

The first thing your patient wants you to do is to listen to her, and hear her out. You can then offer your alternative point of view, but be prepared to put your head on the chopping block and, if possible, try to make sure you are coming from a position of understanding.

An example I will give you is a patient who always comes in and says, "My pain feels like it would benefit from ultrasound". I generally say to this patient, "Well, let's assess your problem, and then I can tell you what's wrong, and once we have worked out what's wrong we can treat you with either X or Y".

THE PHYSIO IS ALWAYS RIGHT. RIGHT?

I don't always need to be right, or to have all the answers. If a certain method of treatment is not working, I'm very open with my patient. As a rule I make a provisional diagnosis in the first consultation, and begin some treatment or education at the first appointment. If I find that within two to three consultations we're not getting the results we need, I will be very honest with the patient, and let him know that we might not have found out what the problem is. The patient is generally quite happy with this, as it shows that I care enough about him and his condition to be thinking hard about the best way to help him.

The worst thing you can do is give up. When I'm treating patients with a difficult problem that requires medication, imaging, or a referral to a GP or specialist, I do not consider this to be a failed venture. My job as their physio is to help them find out what is wrong in their body.

Some of my most satisfying consultations have been long discussions with patients who are in severe pain and are quite distressed. I listen to them describe how the problem is affecting their lives, and after understanding their problem and doing some tests, I let them know that their potential problem is X. If X is not something I can treat and reduce their pain, I let them know the plan of attack. For example, see your GP, have this scan, if the scan shows this you need to proceed with this type of treatment, and so on. This gives patients great reassurance and hope, as they walk out of the treatment room with knowledge and information about their condition that they did not have before. They are empowered, educated, and aware of the next step they need to take in their journey to get out of pain. Even though I sent them elsewhere, they still got what they needed from me.

WHAT DO PATIENTS HATE MOST?

In my experience, patients hate two things more than anything else. It is not you causing them pain, not the fact you have to tell them you don't know what is wrong with them, and it has nothing to do with your clinical repertoire.

The first of the two things is if you are significantly late for their appointment. When I say *significantly late*, this is completely subjective. To gauge what your threshold for waiting for an appointment is, go and see your GP. Grab the 15-year-old magazine, have a seat in the waiting room, and see how long it is before you're looking at your watch. My experience is for many people this threshold is about 15 minutes.

The second thing I believe is a more serious offence than the first. What happens when you go the GP and you're talking to her about your latest medical issue and she doesn't even look at you? She taps away furiously at her computer, without making eye contact. Is she even listening to you? Sometimes she will look up and momentarily make eye contact, but you're fairly sure that most of what you just said has been ignored.

We all want to be listened to, and if your patient is paying you to listen it does pay to make eye contact to reinforce that she has your undivided attention. This will significantly improve your ability to quickly form a trusting relationship, which will allow you to achieve better results.

HOW TO HANDLE A DISSATISFIED PATIENT

WHAT DO YOU DO WHEN YOUR PATIENT WANTS TO BREAK UP WITH YOU?

"You don't need me to come back, do you?"

This was a phrase recently uttered to me at the end of a consultation. My patient was a lady of about 80 years old who had a stroke a year ago, and was getting back to the point where she was starting to walk well again. We had just discussed starting her off on a gym programme at her local retirement village, and she was feeling pretty happy with herself.

Obviously she felt like she was getting to the point where she didn't feel she needed physio treatment anymore. But the sad thing was that she was nowhere near where she needed to be, and nowhere near as fit as she was before having her stroke. She used to walk for 30 minutes a day, and she hadn't even started walking again!

Her intent was obviously to self-discharge – but why? There could be any number of reasons. Sometimes when people have poor health they get sick of seeing doctors and physios, having tests and booking appointments; they just want to get back to their normal, healthy life. Personally I believe this is the number one reason that a patient wants to self-discharge.

Most young practitioners would consider that it's all down to money, but I have to disagree. As a person who is getting older I'm quite happy to exchange good money for good advice and help – I see this as a fair value exchange. Most people I know over the age of 25 tend to think similarly, unless they are struggling to pay the bills.

SEE! YOU DO STILL NEED ME

This lady clearly didn't think she needed any more help, or that I had anything else I could offer her. So how do you articulate to a patient who doesn't really think she needs your help that she *does* still need your help? You refer to her SEE – her Significant Emotional Event. This concept was taught to me by Paul Wright, a great physio private practice educator.

Our patients don't speak the same language we do. They often don't value the years and years of time we spend refining our advice, assessments, treatments and people skills. They think it just comes naturally. They think about their treatment in terms of what is important to them. Getting a good night's sleep. Being able to get up out of a chair or walk without their knee hurting. Spending time with their family and friends (grandkids are generally a huge driver of older people's decision making), hobbies and friend groups offer great motivation.

Back to my patient. She likes to travel. She had done several overseas trips in the last two years, including some quite exotic destinations that required excellent mobility. How do I appeal to someone who loves travel but doesn't realise she needs to be able to walk for more than 30 minutes in one go to be able to travel again?

Instead of telling her what I would do to help her, I decided to ask her how much walking she did when she went on her last trip. She thought about it, and said she walked for hours a day. I then asked her if her current ability to walk would allow her to go on another such trip. She said no. I then asked her if she wanted to travel again. She said yes. Finally, I said to her that if she wanted to travel again she had to get to the point where she could walk more, and she agreed. After this discussion she was happy to continue treatment.

The real skill of the therapist here is highlighting the person's significant emotional event to her, in a way where she is actively involved in the conversation and can identify the problem herself. Instead of giving her the typical sell on the things I could do to help her, I took a different approach by asking her questions about issues which I knew were important to her. This approach worked far better than selling her a solution.

Try this next time you want to influence someone. Ask meaningful questions relating to her significant emotional event rather than selling your wares. If you can help her realise what is most meaningful to her then your solution will sell itself.

PART
IV

BUSINESS

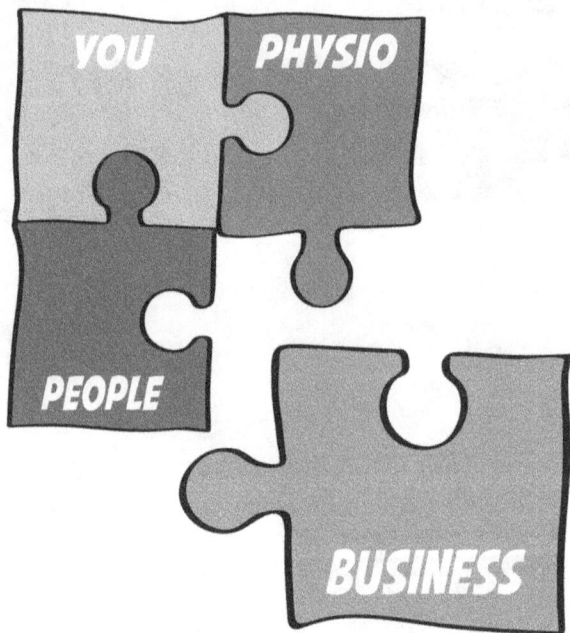

BEING PART OF A STRONG TEAM

THE CLINIC OWNER'S PERSPECTIVE

If you want to be a great employee and work for a clinic where the clinic owner worships the ground you walk on, I have some news for you – you actually have to try to put yourself in her shoes and understand where she is coming from. In this modern world of instant gratification we can't all be practice owners in our twenties, and we need to recognise that we need to learn in our profession, to gain proficiency with our clinical skills, learn how to deal with people and form good practitioner–patient relationships, and – newsflash! – we also need to make our boss happy.

I remember attending a conference where a group of physios and allied health business owners were discussing the differing viewpoints of the employer and the employee within a physio practice. The question was asked, "What does the employer want from their employees?" A young man piped up immediately and said, "My practice owner just wants money". I felt really disappointed by this response, as clearly this young guy had the perception that his boss was only driven by profits. Whether that's true or not, the fact that this young man felt this way reflected poorly on the business.

I do come with a slightly biased opinion as I have been an employer of staff in more recent times. Here is my perspective on the subject. At my clinic, our vision is to make our local region of Redcliffe the healthiest and best place to live in Australia. I have come to this vision over a number of years, mainly due to the fact that I have operated and grown my clinic in Redcliffe over a 14-year period, and the relationships and bonds I have formed with my clients and referrers are so strong that I want the best for our district, and all of the people who live here.

BEING HAPPY, HAPPY, HAPPY

As a business owner, to achieve my vision I need three cogs in the machine to be functioning smoothly. I require:

- happy patients
- happy staff
- a financially happy business model.

I find that unless these three criteria are satisfied the clinic is not running optimally. Let's have a look at each of these.

HAPPY PATIENTS

Most practices will be highly focused on satisfying the patient, which makes perfect sense. If we do not satisfy the patient we will not get repeat business and not build a great profile within our community. Our practice is destined to fail unless we can keep our patients happy. We can achieve this through genuinely caring for our patients, delivering great results, helping them achieve their goals, and generally doing what is in their best interests.

HAPPY STAFF

When it comes to looking after staff, this is the business owner's job. Looking after a team can be like herding cats – there are no hard and fast rules. Effectively I try to form strong bonds with each individual in the team, to try to understand where they are coming from, their background, their lifestyle, their goals and dreams, and also their personality type. This helps me determine the best method of communication to use with them to achieve a win–win result with all communication. I must stress that I'm always after a win–win result when I'm dealing with my staff.

I need to let my staff know that they are valued. I need to give them the appropriate training to deal with clinical situations, interpersonal dealings with patients and fellow team members, and help them achieve their ambitions. I am proud at this stage that although we have had team members come and go, our culture and vision both stay strong, and our team – which currently stands at 15 people and is still very much growing – buys into the vision, and they feel they are achieving their goals working at Scarborough Physio and Health.

HAPPY FINANCES

The final cog in the machine, a financially happy business model, is something that, to be honest, the staff and patients don't really know or care much about. But, for the business owner it is vital. Every day I feel like the head of a family at work. It's my job to make the decisions that result in my team members being fed and clothed and having a roof over their heads. How does this responsibility make me feel? I feel empowered, driven, and filled with purpose. I genuinely care for the members of my team – they are my work family. I am loyal to them, and I really value their loyalty in return.

I put so much time into understanding where my people are coming from that sometimes I get upset when I feel that members of my team are not reciprocating in this way. I feel valued as a boss and a fellow team member when my team members try to understand my situation, and why I need the business to make a profit. Without the business making a profit we are all out of a job. If this happens I have failed in my vision to make Redcliffe the healthiest and best place to live in Australia. I want my staff to be well paid at all times, but not at the expense of the business being profitable; after all, the business remaining profitable is the only thing keeping it going.

I love my job, my business, my team and my patients. If my business became unprofitable I would have to find another way to make a difference. For this reason, sometimes I have to make decisions based predominantly on the business remaining profitable. There are large overheads to running a business as well, such as buying or renting a premises, paying staff salaries and other costs (remember this if you are an employee: the fees you take in are not 100% profit in your boss's pocket).

I would urge staff members to try to understand their boss and why they make the decisions they do. Only then will you be a truly great employee.

CHAPTER

19

IDEAL CLIENTS AND RAVING FANS

There is one sure fire way to succeed in business: to really under-stand the profile and needs of your ideal client. *But in a physio busi-ness we treat everybody, you say, how can we narrow down to only one type of client? Wouldn't this backfire on us and cause us to lose the busi-ness of the people who aren't our ideal clients?*

I will give you an example of how this works. When I was 23 years old I was living it up. I had my own business, had just bought a house, was taking some great holidays, and had a great group of friends who I used to hang out with. But something was missing – a beautiful woman to share my life with. I started to think about this woman, and her qualities. I wanted her to be intelligent, independ-ent and focused on having a great career. I also wanted her to be a caring and compassionate person with family values, a sense of fun, a real drive to live a great life, and a person who is warm and loving. And just to top it off, I was also after a stunner: a tall, leggy, blonde-and-blue-eyed beauty would do me very nicely! If you have ever met me you would know that with these requirements I

159

would have to equip myself with some excellent conversation and rapport-building skills to find this perfect woman, and if I found her I would definitely be punching above my weight.

Fast forward 12 years and – guess what! – I found her, married her, and the rest is history! I found my ideal partner, and I found her by knowing what I wanted in a person. I do believe in the law of attraction, in that if you know what type of people you want to attract, there are forces that result in you generally finding these people, one way or another.

A great business mentor of mine, Brad Flynn from Actioncoach, always tells me, "Nick, you get the people you deserve". Brad, you are right (as always).

WHO ARE YOUR IDEAL CLIENTS?

When you are searching for your ideal clients you need to know who they are. You can start to build a profile of your ideal client with a series of very simple steps:

1   **What type of clients do you like working with most?**
    It could be that you enjoy treating people with a certain type of condition, or people of a certain age group, demographic, hobby or occupation. You may prefer working with men or women. And the list goes on …

2   **What types of clients use your services?** Talking physio, we are generally looking for people who suffer pain, injury or mobility problems. I would generally say that I enjoy treating people who want to live an active life but are restricted by pain. My ideal clients are active women in middle age – it's really frustrating for them when their back pain stops them from chasing their grandkids around.

3   Consider the 80/20 principle, which says that 80% of your business will come from 20% of your clients. My favoured demographic are also great referrers. Once I help them, they tell their friends, kids, parents, and they even book their husband in, as they are sick of him whinging about his pain and not doing anything about it. Of all of the patients you treat, if you track who they were referred by closely you can generally trace them back to your ideal clients, who sing your praises to anyone who will listen

WHERE DO THEY HANG OUT?

The next exercise when it comes to your ideal clients is to work out where you can find them in their greatest numbers. You generally need some local knowledge for this; either that, or a simple method is to actually ask your ideal client questions such as:

- "Which gym do you go to?"

- "What is your favourite restaurant/coffee shop?"

- "Which doctor do you go to?"

- "Where do your kids go to school?"

- "Where do you get your groceries from?"

You can see how varied the questioning can be, and the information you receive will be invaluable. From this, you can build up a great network of businesses you can approach to see how you might be able to build a strategic alliance, which is essentially you helping their customers in return for promoting their products or services to customers of yours who may benefit from doing business with your strategic partner.

For example, I have an incredible personal trainer. He is one of the most inspirational people I know. His name is Jake McLuskie and his business is called Positive Existence Personal Training.

I have trained with him weekly for the last five years, and he keeps me in good shape. Jake and I have a strategic alliance: when a patient of mine wants to get fit I refer her to Jake to do his bootcamps, and conversely when one of his clients hurts herself he refers her to me to get fixed and back exercising. People often joke that we have a "revolving door" of business – his team break them, I fix them up, only for him to break them again! But you would not believe how happy our mutual patients are – they are VIPs, with two awesome businesses looking after them. They feel like rockstars with an entourage and people at the ready, waiting to help them with their every need.

So start thinking about who your ideal clients are and build a profile of them that includes age, sex, family situation, work status, location, hobbies, local businesses they shop with, and more. The greater the detail, the better you'll be able to target them.

CREATE RAVING FANS

In any business the Holy Grail of relationship building is learning to build loyalty among your client list. Loyal patients are a pleasure to deal with – they actively seek out your services, the professional relationship you have with them transcends the traditional dominant–subordinate relationship that often dominates practitioner–patient health services, and you both feel a sense of achievement and satisfaction when you meet, often with great results for both of you.

THE LOYALTY LADDER

Let's have a look at the Loyalty Ladder. This is a concept I learned about from Brad Flynn, my good friend and business coach, who works for the company Actioncoach, which was founded by dynamic Brisbane entrepreneur Brad Sugars. (Seems that to be great in business you have to be named Brad!)

The rungs of the loyalty ladder are:

- Rung 1: Suspect

- Rung 2: Prospect

- Rung 3: Shopper

- Rung 4: Customer

- Rung 5: Member

- Rung 6: Advocate

- Rung 7: Raving fan.

I will now describe each rung on the Loyalty Ladder, and how these rungs relate to a health business.

Rung 1: Suspect – someone in your target market
A suspect is someone who has never heard of your business – they don't know you from a bar of soap. For people working in the physio industry, this includes people who don't even know what physios do. It may be surprising to you, but most people in the community actually have no idea what a physio does, or how they do it. Suspects don't know a physio can help them with their lower back pain. They just want to get rid of their pain; they are not thinking about physio services at all. Suspects ask their family and friends what they should do. Initially they might go to their GP or local pharmacy and get some advice and painkillers. Their GP then suggests that maybe physio could help. This person then becomes a …

Rung 2: Prospect – someone who contacts you
The prospect is now looking around for a physio. The GP may have recommended a certain physio, the person may now be Googling

for a physio in his area, or may have driven past a physio clinic, or his friend may have had good results with a particular physio.

What chance is there that the prospect will choose you? If you have a good reputation and have made contact with your local GPs, if you have a good internet presence, if you have a clinic in a prominent location, or if you have a good reputation in the community, you are in the running for the prospect to choose your service.

In the last 20 years the world of healthcare has changed dramatically. Before the age of freely available and easily accessible information the patient would go to his GP, who would tell him what he needed to do. Invariably the patient would do exactly what the GP told him to. These days, things are different. When the patient feels the first pang of pain, he goes straight to the internet. He is then instantly overloaded with information about what he should do. Your prospect could seek physio or a multitude of other services, all of which he can find online.

Good news! This prospect has chosen your clinic; a good friend who you helped with her problem three months ago has recommended you. A referral from a friend is a strong recommendation. You now have an opportunity to move this prospect further up the Loyalty Ladder, to …

Rung 3: Shopper – someone who purchases once

The shopper is defined as someone who comes into your premises but is not yet a customer; he has not yet purchased your service. I will tweak the concept of a shopper to suit a health-based business. I define a shopper as a patient who uses a clinic's services once, and then does not return. It's extremely rare that people come into your clinic and then do not buy your service. They have racked up the courage to call your clinic and make an appointment, and then to get in their car, and then walk through the door of your clinic – they are not going to turn back now. But what you do next will either leave them as a shopper or move them up to being a customer.

If shoppers do not return it is generally for one of three reasons:

- Reason one is a reason you would not expect: it is all to do with **their circumstances**. They are just passing through, are from out of town, are staying with a family member, or are leaving to go interstate or overseas. They use your service, are happy with the service, but their individual circumstances prevent them from coming back.

- Reason two is that **you didn't satisfy their needs**. The main problem here is likely that you didn't listen to them, you didn't satisfy their main reason for seeking your services, and they feel that you don't understand or care about them and their problem. If you tell someone to rebook and within a couple of weeks you haven't seen them again, alarm bells should ring. More about this later.

- Reason three is **you didn't recommend that they return**. From my perspective, this is an even worse mistake than reason two. I can count on one hand from the 8,000-plus patients I have treated over the years the number who I know will be completely better after one treatment. A mistake that young therapists often make is discharging a patient from their care too soon. As a young therapist you often feel that your patient's recovery will take care of itself. In the health professions we are generally caring people, and we can make the mistake of thinking too much about our patient's bank balances. We are scared to ask them to come back. Do you want to know what the patient is thinking? *My problem isn't fixed yet. I can't believe the physio didn't ask me to come back. Don't they care about fixing my problem?* Think about this.

Do it right, and the patient moves up to ...

Rung 4: Customer – someone who purchases more than once

I consider a customer of my practice to be a patient who has seen through their course of treatment. As a very rough guide I often say that it takes me five consults with patients to really get to know them as a person, and to really understand their problem. Many patients have almost recovered by their fifth session and some have quite a way to go, depending on the problem.

The customer stage is all about solidifying the relationship, helping the patient get out of pain and to reach some of her more immediate goals (which may include better sleep and better movement), and avoiding some negative consequences such as taking pain medications or being off work.

A mentor once told me about something called the "rule of three", which can help to build a relationship. You should remember three personal details about a patient (which might include family members' names and situations, their hobbies, their goals, or even their favourite sporting team), and you should reveal three things about yourself, obviously while maintaining professionalism. Would you like to know the key topic I connect with my patients over? The winner, by a fair margin, is family. Nothing beats family. Our families are the most important people in our lives, and I love finding out about my patients' family situations – who is in the family, how old they are, what their situations are, where they are located. You can learn lots about a person when she starts talking about her family. After all, ours is a family practice – the vast majority of our patients also refer their families, but they only do this once they are a customer, and not before.

Once you start asking these types of questions of your patients, you establish the fact that you genuinely care about them as a person. This genuine care is the absolute cornerstone of our profession. The most important concept in this book is that you must display genuine and heartfelt care for your patients. People don't care how much you know until they know how much you care. Once your patient knows how much you care, they become a ...

Rung 5: Member – someone who feels like they belong
A member of your practice is a customer who returns for a second episode of care for either the same complaint or a different complaint after you have finished helping her with her initial problem. She may continue on with you straight after you have helped her with her first problem, or you may not see her for a year after you have seen her for her initial course of treatment. The bottom line is that you have helped the patient enough for her to have thought of you when she needed help with another problem which has caused her pain. The better you remember her, her family, the problem you treated her for, and the issues you connected over, the more of a member this person becomes. You are becoming her trusted pain and injury adviser, an expert she can turn to when she needs help, she has confidence in you, and she actually enjoys attending her consultations with you. You provide significant value in her life, and you give her hope and empowerment.

The membership stage is often a great stage for you to express your gratitude to your patients. To thank them for their patronage, for their loyalty to you, you can articulate that you value the professional relationship you have with them and you enjoy helping them. I've found that patients will generally receive this gratitude warmly, and with humility. Too often in private practice our patients believe we see them as just a number, or, in a physio's case, a knee or a lower back. If you tell your patients that your professional relationship with them means more than this, the bond strengthens.

At this stage, a member of your clinic often will move themselves up another rung on the Loyalty Ladder, to ...

Rung 6: Advocate – someone who sells you to their friends and family
The difference between members and advocates is their ability to sing your praises within the wider community. I see many members of my clinic long after I have fixed their problem. When I meet them in the street they come up to me, thank me for having fixed their problem, and talk to me about all the great things they are doing in their lives now. Things they couldn't do before they found me. This gives me a great deal of satisfaction. However, it's only in more recent years I have plucked up the courage to say to them, "If you know anyone else who may be going through similar pain to what you were going through when I first met you, please let them know that I would be happy to help".

The failure of members to become advocates often rests on the shoulders of the physio. If we don't ask, we don't get. Patients can't necessarily assume that we want them to refer us their family and friends; after all, we are busy practitioners and often we have long waiting lists. Some of my patients don't think I'm even able to take on any more new patients!

Make sure that you are the one who is solely responsible for transforming your members into advocates. The best reward your patients can give you is a personal recommendation to their family and friends. When patients can't stop referring you to people, they become a …

Rung 7: Raving fan – someone who can't stop selling for you
Here we are – the Holy Grail! These incredible people make your job easy – they are effectively doing your marketing for you. But how did they get to this stage? Did you give them awesome treatment and fix them really quickly? Did you build a great relationship with them? Did you show genuine care and listen to all of their concerns and problems? No doubt you have done all of these things. But there's generally one extra thing you have done for these people, and you may not even know it. You helped them out in a time of great need. You may have been present during a difficult

part of their life, you may have squeezed them into your schedule at short notice, before or after hours, or during your lunchtime. You may have written a letter for them which they really needed, you may have diagnosed a problem that no other professional had been able to diagnose. Whatever you have done, you have left one hell of an impression on them.

Advocates walk around looking for your next customer: "You have a sore back too? Well, you should *definitely* go and see Nick – in fact, I think I have one of his cards on me … here you go."

How do we get more advocates singing our praises? Simple – do more remarkable things for your patients. Be as remarkable as you can. *Always* be thinking about how you can best help your patients, and they will repay your care and attention.

HOW TO SELL YOURSELF TO A PATIENT

So let's talk about that topic that we all hate to discuss: the lovely topic of sales. I used to think you were either a born salesperson or you were not, but this was just another one of my unfounded limiting beliefs that I have been able to completely re-programme over the last 10 years.

Whether we like it or not, if you are working in a customer service profession *you are a salesperson*. Even doctors, lawyers and medical specialists are salespeople. How is this, you may ask? These highly valued professionals have something they want to sell – their services – and they are selling their services to people who want to buy – their clients.

Selling is basically a transfer of value. For a sale to take place and both parties to be happy with the transaction the value exchange needs to be fair. Interestingly, people place different amounts of value on different goods or services. I once treated a guy who said he would pay me $5,000 to fix his problem, and on the flip side I have treated many people (who are generally sent to me on a

Medicare referral) who wouldn't be in my consultation room if they had to pay one cent for my advice.

One of the reasons many of us are scared of selling is due to negative pre-existing beliefs we have around our mental picture of who a salesperson is. My bet is that when you close your eyes and think of a salesperson the image you conjure up is that of a used car salesperson, and the word associated with that image is "sleazy". If you didn't have that image in your mind's eye beforehand then you definitely do now. Society has fuelled this negative belief over many years. Poor experiences with people selling things like solar power, mobile phone plans, and even salespeople collecting for charities have all given us certain feelings of frustration, guilt, anger, shame and other feelings.

So when I say that we are all salespeople, many of you will be offended. This is only natural, and I make no apologies for this – your development in this life will sometimes be uncomfortable, and you must get used to this from time to time as you need to acknowledge your beliefs are only your version of the truth, as mine are also.

When I started thinking about selling being a fair exchange of value it definitely made things easier for me as a professional. I see that there is a significant correlation in our profession between the fear of selling and the feeling that we don't value our time and expertise enough when delivering our consultations as physios.

As a physio, once I started to see my patients achieve better and better results over the years, I became more comfortable with selling them my consultations. These views of mine expanded as I saw all the different ways that various health professionals were helping these patients, and made it easy for me to add different services to our clinic, including massage, custom orthotics, pilates, acupuncture, psychology, and even some more alternative professions such as kinesiology. I saw people with different conditions benefitting from all these different services, and to this day when I see patients

I'm thinking about all the different services we offer which will help them reach their goals quicker and achieve a more permanent result for them in terms of finding the cause of their pain, getting out of pain quickly, and staying that way.

FAB SELLING

A good way for me to give you a light introduction to some sales concepts is something called "features, advantages, benefits" selling, or FAB selling. As physios we are great at talking about the features of physiotherapy; for example, "I am mobilising your L5-S1 vertebra". This is a feature. A feature is important to you but not that important to your patients as they don't really understand it.

Let me explain using the mobilising of the L5-S1 vertebra example.

So the feature is that you as the physio can mobilise the L5-S1 vertebra. The advantage (over, say, chiropractic) is that this treatment achieves the same benefit freeing up the back as a chiropractic manipulation without the risk and pain, and the benefit is that your patient will be able to move and bend better after you do this technique with him.

People don't buy features, they don't even buy advantages – they buy benefits.

Another concept from my business coach Brad correlates with people buying benefits. It's called "WIIFM" – this stands for What's In It For Me?

Brad believes that when people are interacting with businesses they are walking around and in their heads repeating "WIIFM, WIIFM, WIIFM". The potential customer is looking for the real benefit in the service we and competing health professionals offer.

We need to get really good at articulating the benefits of physiotherapy to our clients. A feature of physiotherapy is that we are the best of the allied health professions when it comes to assessing and diagnosing soft tissue problems in our clients. The advantage of being great with assessment and diagnosis is that we give our patients clarity in what is actually wrong with them. The benefit of this is that we can do things to help get them pain free in the shortest amount of time possible, and help keep them pain free by giving them advice and exercises to keep them going well, so the pain doesn't just come back straight away.

Can you see how articulating what we do for our patients in an FAB style is more compelling than just telling them what we do?

Benefits are also very specific, and bring back Paul Wright's significant emotional event philosophy, and once you get to know the patient and what is important to him it makes it much easier to sell him on the benefits of your service.

Exercise: FAB selling to your ideal client

Think about who your ideal client is and what problem you solve for them (do they have low back pain, etc.)

Write down their name.

Now consider one of the ways you help them – it may be a treatment technique, an exercise, advice, a referral, or something else.

What is the feature of this intervention? Write it down.

What is the advantage of this intervention? Write it down.

And finally, what is benefit to the patient of this intervention? Write it down.

Now when you look at your list, you will understand the difference between a feature, advantage and benefit.

Next time you catch yourself speaking to your patient about a feature you are giving them, make sure you translate this into the advantage (why it is better than the alternative) and the benefit (the ultimate result the patient gets) to them.

CHAPTER

20

HANDLING THE MONEY SIDE OF THINGS

TALKING ABOUT MONEY

A great mentor of mine once told me that money finds its way from people who value it least to those who value it most. The bottom line is if money is not among your highest values it will not be something you focus on nor attract in abundance.

WHAT ARE YOUR MONEY BELIEFS?

The concept of money beliefs is often a taboo subject, not only in health or business but in life itself. I have found this topic to be one of the biggest and most common negative beliefs that holds back physios in private practice and stops us from succeeding more in life. Most of us aren't even aware in our lifetimes that this is an issue as our beliefs on this sensitive topic are formed in childhood and only major happenings in our lives alter our beliefs to any great degree.

So let's talk about your specific attitudes and beliefs towards money. Are you a spender, saver, or do you wish money wasn't necessary at all? Did you grow up not wanting for anything, or having to scrimp and save for everything you wanted as a child? Did your parents tell you "money doesn't grow on trees"? Do you live paycheque to paycheque, and live for the weekend and the next big restaurant opening in your favourite night spot? Or do you believe in investing? What do you invest in? How did you come to this decision that this was the best way to invest?

MY MONEY BELIEFS AND HOW THEY TRANSFER TO BUSINESS

I will give you some insight into my money beliefs and how they have changed over my life so far. When I was growing up we didn't see much money. Growing up in a poor suburb in the country town of Toowoomba, Queensland, money was not really that much of an issue to us. We enjoyed going to the corner store to buy some lollies or hot chips, and my parents used to reward us with pocket money for completing weekly tasks, which we put away as savings. The way that you learn about money when you are young has a significant way of shaping how you think about money as you get older and become an adult. My overarching beliefs about money were that we didn't have much, but we had enough and never wanted for anything. Looking back at my childhood I believe this was quite a good way to live. My Dad stressed about losing his job lots, which I suppose was warranted, being a large, single-income family growing up during a time of recession in the 1980s and 1990s. Despite us not having much money, my parents still prioritised sending my brothers and me to the best schools possible, as they valued education highly, and this has flowed over to my belief system. During my later school and university years I always had part-time jobs and developed a good work ethic. I believed that to earn money you had to work hard, as most of the people I saw who were earning money achieved this through hard work.

I remember the thrill of starting at Scarborough Physio in Brisbane. I had just purchased the business, and when you are a young physio owning a business you definitely learn to manage your finances. Some of my childhood money beliefs served me well in the early years, when money was tight.

Keeping overheads low was my key to success in business in those early years. I did not have to earn much as long as I kept my overheads low – as long as I earned enough to pay the bills and take an average wage out of the business I felt this was a good way to start my business career. I was getting a good flow of new patients referred from the medical centre in which I was working, and so I could generally concentrate on looking after my patients, making sure I was on top of the finances, and everything else fell into place – so much so that I was able to buy my first house after having worked for only six months. Looking back, it was probably a purchase that I made too soon, but due to the low costs of running the business I could manage it.

As the years passed my business grew and I saw more patients, but the cost of doing business also grew. Growing a health business while keeping it profitable is a challenge, one I still face today.

In my personal life I tend to be a decent saver of money, but some poor stock market investment decisions just before the Global Financial Crisis in my mid twenties has affected my confidence with investing. My money beliefs are that you generally have to be quite careful with money, and you should allow yourself to spend when it comes to things like holidays, but I try not to waste money on small, everyday things. I always look for specials in the supermarket, I buy petrol on the cheap days, I enjoy going to op shops when I need a business shirt or pair of slacks, and I make my own lunch every day. Combine that with the fact that I try to have an overseas holiday with my wife every year and I enjoy property investing and have a decent property portfolio, and you can see I have some quite unique and unusual money beliefs.

YOUR PATIENTS JUST WANT FAIR VALUE

I'm getting to the most important point and the purpose of this discussion: your money beliefs are not the same as your patients' money beliefs. It's very dangerous to project your money beliefs onto your patients in a clinic setting. Your clients' finances are none of your business. I will explain.

As a young physio you never really have large amounts of money to spend. A good number of the patients you will see in private practice are older than you. They have been working for years in various careers and are generally quite well established. People come from many walks of life, and we can never assume anything about anyone. A big issue I tend to see in young health practitioners is underconfidence and a tendency to undervalue their time and their intervention in private practice, where customers pay a fee for what is effectively nothing more than your time. After being a physio for more than 10 years I now realise that time is more important than money, because it is really the only commodity that you can never get back in life, and it is precious above all. But I didn't realise this at the start of my career, and many young physios have not yet realised this truth. At the start of your career you have ample time and little money, but as we age this ledger tends to skew, and many of our patients, especially those getting older and in severe pain, value their time greatly, and will spend money to get back time (in terms of their pain-free physical state).

When you are a sole practitioner you have to do everything, which includes asking your patients to pay the bill at the end of the consultation. Unless you have worked in retail or a profession where you have to ask customers for money, this can be quite confronting, especially if you feel that you have chinks in your clinical armour. We can assume things like *my patient can't afford my fee, I must be overcharging, I can't book the patient again too soon*, and other negative thoughts based around money. But guess what your patient is thinking? *I hope my practitioner will listen to me, I hope he can help, I just want to get out of pain; let's fix this problem as quickly as possible.*

If you begin to project your money beliefs onto your patients, they will feel this projection and might become nervous. It will make them start to think about their back pocket, and potentially bring into question whether they are getting good value for their hard-earned money. If you believe your service is too expensive, so will they.

Can you see how your money beliefs and your patients' expectations of your service are incongruent if you have these negative money beliefs? Your patients just want you to help them; more often than not they are happy to pay your fee, but on one condition – your service must provide fair value to them. This includes you addressing the main problem they came to you for, which might be getting out of pain, getting a diagnosis from you, getting a plan for how to recover from their ailment, or exercises and advice for how to self-manage their condition.

VALUING YOURSELF, YOUR TIME AND YOUR SKILLS

Not charging a fair fee for a great service with great outcomes and results is a big chink in the armour of our profession and has been for some time. We are being overtaken by chiropractors, naturopaths, homeopaths, myopractors, massage therapists, exercise physiologists and personal trainers in the way in which we confidently and ethically sell our services. Different physios and health practitioners charge different fees. At this moment one of my mentors is charging $850 per hour at his physio clinic. Some of you may say, "How is that possible?", and, "People won't pay that". Well, *most* people won't pay or can't afford this fee. But he operates in a very affluent inner Brisbane suburb, and his service is not for everyone. He has found his niche, and he provides massive value within his niche. He helps people with very difficult problems, his approach is very unconventional, and he gets great results with his clients. He has been a great influence on me, and he has encouraged me above all to place high value on the service I offer and on what I sell, which is my time.

When you sell your time, which is the most precious commodity as you can't get it back, you have to place high value on it. If you treat people for a very low cost, and you are constantly discounting and having to negotiate on your fee, you get involved in price wars, which is always a race to the bottom.

Many clinics offer their services as being the "cheapest" around. But put yourself in the consumer's shoes. Say you have a very difficult problem that you need surgery for. Do you want to see the cheapest surgeon and negotiate on price? Is the cheapest surgeon going to give you the best outcome?

We must value our service and our time more as a profession. If we don't, we will quickly become disillusioned and go and find some other career which rewards us more for our many years of learning and hard work.

Learn to value yourself, your time and your skills more.

21

PHYSIOS AND MARKETING

WHY PHYSIOS NEED TO MARKET THEMSELVES

When I use the word *marketing*, what feelings does it bring up for you? Most physios who are not clinic owners shudder in their boots. Our experiences of marketing are generally people we knew at uni who did marketing and business types of degrees and who now work for advertising agencies and big business.

Firstly, I would like to differentiate marketing from advertising. Marketing is your personal (or business) brand and every element of your customers' experience with you; advertising is simply one medium for delivering a message to a potential client. My initial thought about marketing was similar to yours: "I am a professional; why do I need to market myself?" I assumed I could just start a clinic and the customers would flow. Where they would flow from, I didn't know.

As an employee in a physio or allied health clinic, marketing is a very important string to your bow. Would you believe that clinic owners regard skills and experience in marketing yourself very highly when considering a new hire? I want to know as the clinic owner that my therapists value their ability to build a caseload, and know that this needs to be done through building their profile and building solid relationships with existing and potential clients in the community.

Your ability to market yourself initially revolves around your desire to help your initial clients as much as you can, do a great job with them, wow them, and not only meet but exceed their expectations. The more clients you can turn into raving fans, the more they will talk about you in the community and refer their family members and friends to you.

Many young physios I have mentored and met over the years have a real fear when it comes to marketing. Sometimes I sense that we as a profession believe that our degree is a ticket to success, and that we should be able to sit in our consult room and attract streams of loyal clients without having to lift a finger.

Now this could not be further from the truth. The allied health sector is becoming increasingly competitive, and developing a reputation in your community for excellence takes time and is extremely important to do if you want to attract the type of patients to your clinic that you would enjoy treating.

HOW TO BECOME KNOWN IN YOUR COMMUNITY

It's rare that you can attract these patients by sitting quietly in your consulting room. When a new physio starts at my clinic, my goal with them is to help them to be known in our community as rapidly as possible. This involves firstly helping them to get to know our whole team, who are their best source of referrals. A really good way to do this is to have a new physio in your clinic treat all of the other staff when they get aches and pains, especially the reception staff. If you are a new physio to the clinic in which you are working, this is a great strategy – guess who books your appointments?

The second way to become known in your community is through your clinic's existing client database, and there are several strategies to do this, many of which involve a smooth transition from the previous physio in the role to the new physio, if this is your situation. This can be as simple as a phone call to the patients who the physio you are replacing used to see, to introduce yourself and see how they are going, to a group email to the database, or some high-quality information-based posts to either an email database or Facebook page or group.

The third way to become known is through an introduction to your existing referrers. I ask all of my physios to go and meet our referrers in person and take offer cards with them. These people include GPs, specialists, gyms, other health professionals, and local businesses with whom we cross refer. I make sure the offer is a strong offer – for VIPs we offer them a free consultation with our new physio (a VIP is not only a great customer but a great referrer), and for clients of our VIPs we have a less strong offer – either a discounted initial consultation, or a value add (more services as part of the initial consultation).

The fourth way to become known is through new referral sources. It is advantageous when you as a physio have your own referral sources; for example, the school you went to, clubs and societies you are a part of, and other connections you have in your community. A tip from an employer – mention this during your job interview and it will put you in the box seat. I know I would hire a skilled physio who fits my team culture with a ready-made network of referrers in a second!

The fifth and final way to become known in your area is speaking to any of the groups we have just mentioned. There is nothing that builds trust quicker than speaking in front of a group of potential clients or referrers and giving them great-value informa-tion, as well as answering their questions. I aim to do one speaking engagement a month.

FINDING YOUR NICHE

So back to marketing. Marketing is all about your personal brand as a therapist, and your brand within the clinic you work in. One ele-ment of marketing many physios have trouble with is their niche. Choosing a niche can be scary, as by choosing a niche our natural concern is that we will eliminate the potential to see all other clients outside this niche.

Some common niches are sports, pilates, women's health, and body segments; for example, back pain or shoulders.

The way I have got around this problem and still chosen a niche is by giving myself time as a generalist (not that I can now say I am a "specialist" – we have to be careful of using this term in our profes-sion) to determine which type of complaints I like treating, and for me it was the more challenging long-term, chronic and severe pain presentations I really enjoy, as people with these problems need a very thorough and expert approach to help them recover.

So now I tell people that my special area of interest is chronic, severe and long-term pain. Patients who suffer these problems iden-tify with this immediately, and during my initial consultations with them I feel I get really good commitment from them, as they already have a high level of trust in me and how I can help them, which is transferred to them by the person who referred them to me.

You shouldn't place pressure on yourself to develop a niche too close to the start of your career. Instead, consider what you as a physio can offer your ideal client. As younger physios tend to spend more time with their clients, this one-on-one uninterrupted time is a great opportunity to advertise to potential new clients.

Similarly, I tend to spend most of my client time in the clinic and my colleagues do external visits to local gyms, hydrotherapy pools and the occasional home visit, and these are all selling points.

* * *

Consider marketing yourself in the ways I have mentioned above. But don't believe you can do it sitting behind your computer – you need to get off your bum and meet people.

Exercise: Finding your ideal clients

Who are the patients you love serving the most?

Write down who these people are and give them a name (potentially the name of your favourite client who fits these criteria).

Next, write down everything you know about them – where do they shop, where do their kids go to school, where do they go to the gym, GP, dentist, hairdresser, and so on?

This will help you know where to start to find more people just like your ideal client.

THE
IMPORTANCE OF
NETWORKING

PROFESSIONAL ISOLATION AND WHAT TO DO ABOUT IT

One of the biggest challenges I have come across in my career is the challenge of professional isolation. Early in my career I learned that physios in private practice are scared of each other. I believe this comes from some innate competitive nature and wanting to be the best at our craft, but also being super nervous about other people potentially being better physios than us. This mentality, which is strong within our profession, drives us towards professional isolation, which in turn feeds our competitive streak.

We all believe we have some "secret" that makes us better than other physios. This causes us to withdraw professionally and do our own thing once we have a solid skillset, for fear of other people challenging the way we do things in our clinical practice which may make us look stupid, and this challenges the very core of who we are individually as physios.

Long ago I let go of the fact that I needed to be the best physio in Australia. I realised that my real passion was the communication elements of our profession, both when training my team and treating my patients. Now certain physios believe the best physios are the best communicators, others believe the best physios have the best manual techniques, some believe the best researchers lead our profession, and others believe it's the innovators and people at the cutting edge of our profession that are leading us forward.

My concern is not whether I'm the best physio but the standing of the physio profession as first-contact practitioners within the community. I want people in pain to really only have one thought when they need help – and that is to see a physio. We are the best people to actually enlighten them and tell them what is wrong in their body, why they are in pain, and how to get better. No other profession does this as completely as we do.

NEVER STOP LEARNING

Based on this being my goal, I realise I am just one physio and I cannot do this alone. For this reason I am a member of the Australian Physiotherapy Association (APA). Why am I a member of the Australian Physiotherapy Association and what do I get out of my membership? When I was young (and if you are a young physio), the main benefit of being part of the APA was access to quality professional development courses throughout the country, and now you can even access professional development online through the APA, sometimes even for no charge. The first five years of your career should really be spent refining your craft and gaining exposure to experts and new concepts.

As we get older as physios we tend to undervalue APA membership as we feel that we have already learned the bulk of the physio techniques we need for our clinical practice. I thought this after my first five years of practice, until I realised that I now needed access to people with similar mindsets to me, to keep me striving to be the best physio I can be and to be led by other pioneers within our profession.

The second you start to believe you are the most awesome physio in the world is the second you are becoming complacent. I have found a cure for this: teaching other physios. The questions physios ask me when I am teaching definitely bring me back to earth, and make me aware of how much more I want to learn about physio, business, communication, and life in general.

BRING IT ALL TOGETHER

So how do you be the ultimate physio?

You need to optimise these four areas of your physio life:

1   **You**

- know who you are
- know where you want to be
- develop a plan to get there

2   **Physio**

- get optimal results, simply
- systematise it
- constant improvement and refining

3   **People**

- understand people
- help people
- positively influence people

4   **Business**

- find patients

- keep patients

- referrals from patients

SO, WHAT NEXT?

Guess what? Information is useless, unless you do something worthwhile with it.

How many times have you read a book or attended a course, and come away all inspired, but then woken up the next day and done nothing? Well, I don't want to let you get away with this sort of mentality.

As a physio you need to be constantly learning, and as a profession this tends to be our strong point. Like I have experienced in the past, the majority of the time what holds us back, especially as professionals, is lack of action.

First up, we think we know it all. My business coach Brad Flynn refers to this as "I know". If you have read this book and as you read the chapters you are subconsciously saying "I know" to yourself, your brain does not take in new information.

I will often re-read the same book or even attend the same course as I have before, as I learn new and finer distinctions as I go, due to being in a potentially different state of mind at the time.

The second point – you need to play "above the bar". You must take responsibility for everything that happens in your life, both good and bad. No excuses, no blaming it on other people, or situations out of your control, like the economy, or your competitors. Playing above the bar is something I have struggled with over the years, as it's really easy to blame external circumstances when things don't go your way. But the reality is that if you are not getting the results you want in any element of your life, it's up to you to change this.

A BETTER FUTURE

Change is hard. The first step in making meaningful change in your life is being dissatisfied with the status quo, and the second step is having a vision for a better future.

So what is a better future for you as a physio? Better physio skills? Patients you love treating? More patients? A thriving practice? A team that works together? An environment where you love coming to work every day?

If you believe there is something more to your physio career than the results you are already getting from day to day then I hope *Becoming the Ultimate Physio* has helped you to identify what the next steps in your development should be.

There are plenty of great resources available to help you take that next step. Please check out the free resources available that I have provided for you at www.ultimatephysio.com.au, and should you want to take the next step with me in your development not only as a physio but more importantly as a person, I have courses that can help you do this as well, and you will find more info in the courses section of www.ultimatephysio.com.au.

Finally, please come and be part of Australia's biggest community of physios and physio clinic owners by joining our Facebook groups – one for physios in private practice, one for physio clinic owners. No doubt this book has you thinking, and you will have lots of questions you need answers to, and to have access to hundreds of people just like you and willing to help you find the answers to these questions is a bonus of being a member of our community.

I look forward to helping on your journey of physio success. If you wish to contact me please do so at:

Nick@ultimatephysio.com.au.

My highest value is positively influencing people. As a physio I initially did this through my clients, as a clinic owner I do this through mentoring my team and helping them achieve their goals, and my wish now is to positively influence as many physios and clinic owners as possible, so that we can live awesome lives where we value ourselves greatly and squeeze every last drop out of life.

Thanks for reading and coming on this journey with me.

www.ingramcontent.com/pod-product-compliance
Lightning Source LLC
Chambersburg PA
CBHW060320030426
42336CB00011B/1134